AS ITS PEOPLE
a 90-day challenge

Have happy, engaged, high-performing employees,
who make your company legendary

Joan Elmore

This book is designed to give general information about the subject; however, as laws, regulations, and practices vary from geographical locations, industries, and organizations, and because specific circumstances vary, this book is not intended to serve as legal, financial, or other professional advice.

The reader is responsible for complying with all laws, regulations, and practices of his/her specific area, industry and company; should tailor all the advice in this book to his/her own specific circumstances; should use his/her own judgement about what and how advice in this book applies; and should seek his/her own advisor regarding his/her specific circumstances.

Neither the author nor the publisher assumes any responsibility for any errors or omissions in this book, or for individual results from the use or application of the information contained in this book.

Published by Veronica Press Company, Inc.
Daytona Beach, FL 32119

Printed in the United States

First Edition

To all my coworkers.

You're the best thing about going to work!

contents

Your company is only as good as the people in it.

We've all heard some variation of that saying. And starting today, you and I are going to take it to heart, and work together to help each of your employees have happiness, fulfillment, and high-performance in his/her position.

Your company is going to be an exclusive club, which will only accept and keep members of the highest quality, and will treat its members like VIPs. Getting there is your priority from now on, and we're going to have it all set up and running by the end of this challenge.

You're going to create an environment where people with varied personalities, backgrounds, skills, and values can thrive. You're going to give them a place where they feel cared for, valued, appreciated, and respected. You're going to give them work that challenges them, excites them, and makes them better. You'll help them to learn more, and progress, and use their strengths. And you'll be able to give them all that, no matter what their job description actually is.

And this process is for you too. You'll come out of this with more happiness, and more fulfillment. You'll be able to spend more time on your priorities. You'll have more love for your work. You'll love the people you work with. Your work will be even more meaningful. You'll be able to use it to give back to the world. Your work will help you to achieve your own personal goals. It will make you grow, and progress, and become better.

You won't be the same coming out of this, and neither will your employees. And since massive transformation is the goal, we're cramming a lot into ninety days, but I'm confident that you can do this. Take each of these steps one day at a time. Some are small; they might feel unnecessary. Some might feel too far out of your comfort zone. And they each have a specific purpose.

This isn't the type of challenge that tells you to do one thing, repeat it every single day for ninety days, and collect a prize at the end. You're going to be doing lots of different things. Some on your own time, some at work. Some you'll do once, some you'll repeat every day after you've started. You're going to be layering and layering; action upon action, habit upon habit.

I see amazing changes in your future!

Here's some tips to help you get the best outcome:

This is a workbook. You don't have to treat it gently and read it like a novel. Have a pen out when you go through it each day. Write in it. Mark it up. Each day will give you a checklist of the things you should be doing daily, and there's space to check off each thing as you complete it. At the beginning of each week, there will be a list of things to do at least once a week, with spaces to check those off as you complete them. At the beginning of each month, there will be a checklist of things to do regularly and consistently. Many of the days have sections for you to write in, and at the end of each week there are bigger sections for you to freely brainstorm and write down your ideas.

Don't rush ahead. Take it day-by-day, week-by-week. If you can't stand the suspense and want a preview of what's to come, that's fine, but go back to the current day and do that step, and each one after. After the first week, keep page markers on the page for the current day, and the page for the current week, so you can make sure to complete each action. Once you get to the first month's checklist, add a page marker there too.

You don't have to start this on a Monday. Since all our work schedules vary, I just wrote this to start on any day, whether you're working or not. If you get to a day that asks you to do an at-work-specific thing and it's your day off, just set up a reminder for yourself, so you'll remember to do it the next time you're at work (and you can go back to the page for that day and check it off once you've completed it).

If you change jobs (since this is also for those of you in HR/management positions) at any point after starting the challenge, start the challenge over. That way you can apply each of these strategies at your new job and reap the rewards there.

You'll need to do this with the right attitude. You want to be humble, teachable, friendly, kind, respectful and sincere, or you could sabotage your results.

Consistency is essential. This can't be like a gym membership, or a no-carb diet, or a pledge to stop swearing when you get cut off in traffic. Putting positive things in place for a time and then abandoning them won't go over well with your employees, and could actually bring morale down lower than wherever it was at the start. During each part of the challenge, think about how you can tailor the strategy to fit your organization and make it something you can stick to consistently.

For the next ninety days, you're playing a game. See what you can do, and how good you can get at it.

week 1

day 1

To give your best to your employees, you've got to feel fantastic about you. So we're kicking things off with something to help you get into a specific mindset about yourself:

Whenever you're alone today and you pass or are in front of a mirror, look into it at your reflection and smile.

That's right.

Yes – it's so simple. Yes – it will feel ridiculous. No - you don't want to do it in public. And no – the whole book isn't full of stuff like this.

But today it is, and I promise, it's for your own good. Whenever you're alone in front of a mirror, look at your face in it, and smile.

Repeat this every day for the next 90 days.

day 1 checklist

_____ smile at yourself in the mirror

day 2

Make a list of each person who works for you, and at least one thing you appreciate about him/her. If the size of your company makes it impossible to write down every name, just list the people who work in the same building, or the same department, or the same team, or who interact with you regularly. Like I said yesterday - you're getting into a specific mindset.

day 2 checklist

_____ smile at yourself in the mirror

_____ make a list of your employees and at least one thing you appreciate about each

_____

_____

_____

_____

_____

_____

_____

day 3

Smile at, and greet everyone you pass at work today.

If you're walking by one person at a time, use that person's name. If you try to do this while you approach a group, you'll sound like a crazed robot, so in that case, a general greeting to everyone at once is great.

Look the person in the eyes while you say hello to him/her, and make sure your smile is real by thinking about something funny, or something you're really excited about.

And don't bother asking, "how are you?" unless you've got time to halt, actually listen to the answer, and respond to it.

I'm telling you, this will put you into a great mood, no matter how little you felt like interacting when you woke up today. I started doing this as an employee at one of my jobs, and all the smiles back at me made me feel fantastic about working there with them.

Repeat this every work day for the rest of this challenge.

day 3 checklist

_____ smile at yourself in the mirror

add this if it's a **work day:**

_____ smile at, and greet every person you pass today at work

day 4

Whether or not you ended up doing this yesterday, you're going to do it today, and you're going to be purposeful about it. Ask an employee, "**how are you?**" and then follow it up with the part that most of us (me included) forget to do so much of the time with anybody: **Really listen to the answer, and give a thoughtful response to it.**

No matter how much your employees already know you care, you're going to step up your game during this challenge, and show them even more. And the great news is, it doesn't take grand gestures. You'll make more of an impression with the simple things you do consistently, than turning the office upside-down once a year on Employee Appreciation Day. So this is one little thing you'll do regularly: ask an employee how he/she is doing, really listen to the answer, and give a thoughtful response.

And yes – you're already being pulled apart by people who need you. And yes – you've got fires all over the place waiting for you to put them out. And yes – you could go overboard with this one, like anything else in the world, so this doesn't mean you're going to leave your nine o'clock meeting attendees to spin in their chairs in the conference room while you commiserate with your accountant over his date-gone-wrong. And it doesn't mean you're going to leave your own work to pile up, so you can trek all over the building every day asking people how they're doing and listening to the play-by-play of each person's current situation.

There's a good middle ground to pretty much everything, and you'll walk it in this case too. Do this with care, and your own best judgement, and you probably won't have the chance to do it every single day, with every single employee. So **repeat this at least once a week, with one person** (and switch it up each time, so you eventually do this for everyone you work with), **for the rest of the time of this challenge**.

day 4 checklist

_____ smile at yourself in the mirror

add this if it's a work day:

_____ smile at, and greet every person you pass today at work

_____ ask an employee, "how are you?", listen to the answer, give a thoughtful response

day 5

Want to know a secret?

It just might be the biggest key to employee motivation and engagement, and I think this is what should be the celebrated, previously-buried-in-the-earth-until-its-remarkable-discovery, treasure of our time.

Ready for it? This is huge:

Your employees can use this job to get what they want.

Yep! Let's read it again and let it sink in.

Each of your employees can take this job – that they have right now, working for you – and they can use it to achieve any goal they have for their lives, and have the life they want.

Working for you, at this company, gives them endless opportunities to develop knowledge, skills, character traits, connections, and advantages that will take their life anywhere they want it to go, as long as they *take* all of those things, and use them purposefully, and with a plan.

And you want them to, because here's what you'll get out of it:

Engagement. Motivation. Increased accuracy. Increased output. High performance. Higher profits. Achievement of your company's goals. Achievement of your own personal goals, if you get to where you use all this with your own purposeful plan. Happy employees. Happy customers. A company great people want to work with, and for. A *lasting* company, with a legacy people can't stop talking about.

A company with some secret that people just can't quite figure out. But you'll know it.

And wait a second –

If your employees are using this job to get whatever-it-is they want –

Doesn't that mean they might… *leave* at some point?

Doesn't that mean a bunch of them might fly out of here eventually to become world travelers, or stay-at-home parents, or mountaintop yoga instructors, or to start their own companies?

Yes. It does mean that.

And you want to help them along so they can get to that day, because it will give you a *huge* advantage over all of your competition.

I *promise*, you would rather have people who are happily working for you for a shorter amount of time, than people who are feeling disappointed, bitter and resentful, and giving you decades of service. You will get *so much more* out of each person you have, for however long they decide to stay, if you understand this truth about their job, and help *them* to understand it.

I bet your competition does not understand this. I bet your competition is only focusing on their employees' sales goals, and production goals, and profit goals.

But your employees each have personal goals, and those will nag at them no matter how much their job seems to create a distraction. Make their job a tool instead; make it the factor that gets them to the achievement of their goals, and just watch how much they pay you back.

You're going to start helping your employees with their personal goals during this challenge, and it's going to be so fun, so exciting, and so, so rewarding. I'll give you your first step tomorrow!

day 5 checklist

_____ smile at yourself in the mirror

_____ read both pages of DAY 5, so you'll understand a key strategy to motivated, engaged, and high-performing employees

add this if it's a **work day:**

_____ smile at, and greet every person you pass today at work

day 6

Set up a meeting with each employee, so you can find out his/her personal goals.

Keep in mind going into this, that people will probably be wary about spilling these. As employees, we generally expect that if our bosses found out we have daydreams about anything other than our jobs, it wouldn't turn out well for us.

So here's the rules:

(1) Know already that you're probably going to be given the safe answer, and that you should accept it. Don't freak your employee out and make things uncomfortable by pushing for the "real" thing, or trying to convince him/her that you can be trusted. You'll make this whole thing backfire. Accept the answer you're given.

(2) There can be zero judgement, zero disappointment or anger, and zero negative consequences, no matter what you're told. Your right-hand employee longs to go back to school for something totally different? Or wants to take a year off and find himself by living abroad? Or dreams about starting a business of her own? You aren't going to be ruffled about finding out, because you understand that these things have been there all along, and using them to your advantage instead of fighting or ignoring them is fantastic for you.

(3) You'll want to follow up with each person soon after meeting with them this first time, so they'll know you actually intend to help them. I don't have any way of knowing which day that will fall on, so each step is going to be given over the next few days, and you can just keep the pages marked until you've completed them (with each employee) and can check them off.

Sound good?

Your step for today is to set up the appointment with each employee. Your meetings should only take five to ten minutes max with each person.

Just so no one's imagination runs wild between now and the meeting, give some indication that this isn't about a write-up or a raise. You could have it explained at the time of making each appointment that you're just going to ask each person one question that will help you with something you're considering.

And here's another quick tip: Someone else can set the appointments for you, but if at all possible, *you* should be the one to have these meetings, even if it's your name on the building. That'll make the biggest and best impression, which - like we've established - is going to be wonderful for you.

But if the size of your company makes this impossible, meet with the people who work closest to you, and then arrange for other company leadership to have these meetings with the people who work closely with them.

Just make sure *none* of your employees are left out, no matter their position.

Oh – and pick a goal yourself, and write it down here. You're going to share this one with your employees and let them cheer you on, so pick something you'd want them all to know. So maybe leave out monetary goals. Pick something like running a marathon, or getting a motorcycle license, or hiking a certain trail, or learning another language. You know – something they can all genuinely get behind.

day 6 checklist

_____ smile at yourself in the mirror

_____ pick one of your goals to share with your employees

add this if it's a **work day:**

_____ smile at, and greet every person you pass today at work

_____ set appointments with each employee, to learn their personal goals

day 7

Meet one-on-one with each employee for five to ten minutes max. Say you've been thinking lately that work will be a lot more fun if you're all supporting each other in your individual pursuits of personal goals, and so today you'd just like to find out one thing this employee would love to do or accomplish for him/herself.

You can choose to share your goal right now if you want, if you think it might help your employee to know they don't have to choose something work-related. But either way, and no matter what you're told, remember the rules from yesterday, and when you're given the answer, respond enthusiastically to it, and thank your employee for sharing.

Then explain that you're going to be taking some time to think about how you all can best support each other with the things you want to do, and that you'll be getting back to everyone soon, and then you can end this meeting and repeat it all in the next.

And just - some pointers. Keep your attitude sincere, and kind, and caring, and… casual, if that makes sense. No matter how cool my boss is, and how sure I am that I'm doing a great job, a call in to an office for a one-on-one meeting makes me nervous. So don't be too intense about the whole thing, and make sure you get to the point right away, so no one sits in anxiety while you make small talk.

As soon as the employee leaves, write his/her name and goal down, and some notes about anything elaborated on, so you'll have a reference for later and won't mix people's goals up (you'll be doing more with this later).

day 7 checklist

_____ smile at yourself in the mirror

add this if it's a **work day:**

_____ smile at, and greet every person you pass today at work

_____ meet with each employee and find out one of his/her personal goals

notes & ideas

week 2

week 2 checklist

here's what you'll do at least 1 time this week

_____ ask an employee, "how are you?", then listen to the answer and give a thoughtful response

extra credit

By the time I graduated high school, I already had some crazy ideas about jobs. They were things I'd heard from my friends, from my friends' parents, and even some of my teachers.

Out in the working world, I kept hearing them, and I started sharing them. They sounded like facts, and everyone seemed to know them. But they left me feeling disappointed, discouraged, resentful, and ashamed.

It took me a long time to learn the truth. And just in case you have employees who think the way I used to, here's the link to a video that will call out the myths, and set it all straight:

https://youtu.be/AMwXXrNAffU

Use it to understand and empathize with what some of them might be feeling, going through, or being told, and to get crystal-clear yourself on the truth.

If you'd rather not try to type that messy link into your browser, you can find the video by:

-Going to my YouTube channel, **Clocked-In with Joanie**

-Going to "Playlists"

-Choosing the "Start Here" playlist

-Going to the video called, "**The Truth About Your Job**"

day 8

Take time by yourself to think about the meeting you had with each employee (about his/her personal goal).

You're going to start brainstorming all the ways your company *might* support those goals more. It could be through a schedule change, some remote work, or time off during an event. It could be through some new or additional assignments that would give necessary experience, teach skills, or allow for travel. Or it could be through a different position altogether, or a transfer, or a meet-up with someone you know who could be a mentor or valuable connection.

Don't panic about this, or think you have to sacrifice yourself or your company's best interest to help someone reach his dreams. You're just thinking today about what you *might* be able to do. You aren't making any promises, and you aren't going to do anything rash.

Just think today, and write down your ideas. Then keep thinking and adding to your notes over the next week (on DAY 15 we'll talk about moving forward on any of these if you decide to).

day 8 checklist

_____ smile at yourself in the mirror

_____ brainstorm ways the company *might* help support each employee's goals more

add this if it's a work day:

_____ smile at, and greet every person you pass today at work

day 9

Years (and years) ago, I joined a weight-loss group that would meet together once a week. We'd each weigh in as soon as we walked through the door, and a nice lady would write my number on a little chart and hand it back to me.

And almost immediately after recording our weight, we were all encouraged to share our successes that week. The whole room would explode in clapping and cheers as people would say, "well, I went to a party and I was having so much fun dancing, I only had time for one slice of cake!", or "my mother-in-law was at our house all last week, but I didn't binge or fight with her!" or, "I usually gain during the holidays, but this week I've stayed at the same weight!"

At the very first meeting, I slouched in my chair and looked around skeptically as people went wild for each other. But by the end of it, I couldn't wait to come back. And at my second meeting, I waived my hand around, so I could take a turn celebrating with everyone that I'd taken a walk three times that week. It's genius, really. And it can be so simple for you to use here:

Get all your employees actively supporting each other's personal goals. Even if it turns out that there's nothing else your company can do, this one by itself will be huge.

You could have regular meetings where each person shares his/her personal goal and the things to have completed by the time of the next meeting. Or you can put each name and goal on a big chart, with places for setting personalized benchmarks and marking progress on each person's dream. Or you could do both things, or something different altogether.

Just make sure your plan includes a way to share successes with the whole group, and get everyone celebrating and encouraging each other for the time ahead. And include your own goal in this (the one you wrote down on DAY 6), so your employees can cheer you on too.

So here's your list for today:

(1) Make your plan.

(2) Set up any automatic reminders you need, for whatever preparation this will require.

(3) Put the start date into your calendar.

Don't let yourself get too busy for this. I promise, it's going to be so good for you!

day 9 checklist

_____ smile at yourself in the mirror

_____ keep thinking of ways the company _might_ support each employee's goals more

_____ make a plan to help all your employees actively support each other's goals

_____ set up any reminders you need, for preparation of your plan

_____ put the start date into your calendar

add this if it's a **work day:**

_____ smile at, and greet every person you pass today at work

day 10

One of my friends has had several sales positions at various companies, and one day he explained a practice that a few of the companies had in common.

Managers would meet with the sales team once a week, or once a month, or whatever it was for that particular business, and they'd go over the goals for the next period of time. Sell a certain dollar amount from each of these categories, sell a certain percentage of these items, sell a certain number of these verses those - whatever the goals were.

And they'd pump everyone up with promises. Your commission rate increases to this once you hit this number. You get a bonus of this once your sales reach that. If this many items get sold by the group by this date, you each get a bigger bonus than usual.

Initially, my friend and his coworkers would leave these meetings and sprint their way through the month. They were boldly making calls, or knocking on doors, or approaching everyone who wandered by their store. And they'd celebrate to themselves, and mentally count the money as they got closer to hitting their goals.

But then something would happen, if they did too well too early. The goal would change. They'd be told that they were on track to overshoot their target, and that now to get the prize, they had to continue this trend for the rest of the allotted time.

Does that make sense? If they were doing too well, it was assumed by management that the goal was too low, and it better be moved just out of reach again, or people would stop working as soon as they reached it. Many of the bonuses or higher commissions didn't get paid, because – technically - the goals hadn't been reached, since they were constantly changing.

Sales people were discouraged and frustrated, until they figured out how to make sure they got their bonuses: stop selling as much. If they made a half-hearted effort and scraped by for most of the month, their goal stayed in place, and during the last week they could ramp things up and reach it by a thread. Then their "numbers" were good, and they got their bonus, or whatever they'd been promised.

And even when the sales teams figured out how to hit their goals and get their commissions, their managers still kept them in a constant state of stress and discouragement, by critiquing previous shortcomings and then immediately harping on the next goal, instead of taking time to celebrate the achievements that had just been made.

It created a long, painful spiral. And it all seems so backward, doesn't it? Maybe their managers thought that was the way to show everyone how much more they could do, or maybe they were just following company policy, but either way, it didn't get great results for anyone. Turnover was high, morale was low, two of those businesses ended up closing several locations, another closed an entire division of the company, I've heard through the grapevine that the horizon for each is still gloomy, and I can't help but wonder if their sales strategies had anything to do with it.

Here's the moral of the story:

We've been talking about your employees and their personal goals for the last five days, but today, make sure you stay in the right mindset and have good habits when it comes to helping them achieve the company's goals.

Take time to celebrate their achievements. Don't move right on to talk about the next goal, and don't save your celebrating for only when they've hit the last one exactly. Maybe someone made way more of an effort, or someone else ventured outside of his comfort zone, or another person had a brilliant idea for marketing to a new area that's going to pay off with time. Make a big dang deal about all those things, so you can keep everyone's enthusiasm and energy up.

And once you set a goal, leave it alone. If everyone hits it with thirty days to spare, have a big party, schedule the bonuses or whatever the promised payout was, and then let them see how much more they can do with the rest of the time left. If you still want to set a higher goal at this point, give all the rewards for the first one, and let this be an additional way to earn more.

If, on the flipside, there's two days to spare and everyone is lagging, don't bring the goal down to their level, because that won't help you or any of them either. The only thing that will need to change is how much everyone's doing to work toward it.

So set the goal, determine the reward, and then leave those things alone. Let your employees hit it, let them collect the prize, make them feel fantastic for doing it, and if they come up short, they just need to increase their activity next time, and you will still celebrate the achievements and effort they did make.

If you aren't in the position to change the way sales/company goals are set or managed, and you're also in the position to enforce counterproductive practices, see what you can do to suggest changes to the people who make those decisions. And understand how your employees are feeling, and why it might be an uphill battle as you try to increase everyone's activity levels. Study what other people in your position have done to motivate a sales team with similar challenges. And celebrate successes like crazy.

day 10 checklist

_____ smile at yourself in the mirror

_____ keep thinking of ways the company _might_ support each employee's goals more

_____ read both pages of DAY 10

add this if it's a **work day:**

_____ smile at, and greet every person you pass today at work

day 11

Do something active each day, starting today.

You might already be in the habit of exercising regularly, and if so, that's great! And if you want to challenge yourself a little more, then try some different workouts now and then, or add in stretching, or something like that.

But if you aren't in the habit, don't worry, because I'm not a personal trainer, and this isn't about getting in shape. This is another way to get yourself in the right mindset. You want to have energy, confidence, clarity, and a way to fight off stress, and there's just something about getting physical activity that lights all of us up.

It could be taking a walk, or stretching while you wait for the microwave to finish your popcorn, or doing some arm circles while you watch TV. The specifics don't matter, and you don't have to do the same activity every day. Pick something you *want* to do, something you can do, and the amount of time you can do it on that specific day. Just do *something* active everyday for the rest of the time of this challenge.

bonus: Find a way to do something active at work, even if it's just some stretching every couple of hours. If you're like me and can barely keep your eyes open after lunch, or find yourself aching after a whole day in the same position or using the same repeated motions – this will do wonders.

day 11 checklist

_____ smile at yourself in the mirror

_____ keep thinking of ways the company *might* support each employee's goals more

_____ do something active

add this if it's a work day:

_____ smile at, and greet every person you pass today at work

day 12

I have this memory that's branded into my brain. I'd been at a particular job for several years, and things had become routine. I knew what I needed to get done, so I didn't need direction unless I got asked to do something extra, and that was great with me, because I like my independence. I'd get to work and hunker down, and it was all a nice routine.

But for whatever reason, I had this stretch of time there where I was feeling a little… out of sorts. I was coming in, doing my work, going home, repeating it the next day. And I was starting to feel like it didn't matter to anyone. I just sort of felt lost in the big machine; like a little piece that might not make much of a difference to anything if it fell off.

I didn't say anything about it, but it began to really bother me. I wondered if I was doing enough, or doing well enough. My confidence was sinking, and when I suddenly started making repeated mistakes, I freaked out and took it as a sign that I really wasn't cut out for this job.

Isn't it funny how much we can let ourselves spiral? I don't know what in the world had gotten into me, but at the time it felt like I was right. And one day, out of the blue, my boss paused on his way past my desk, and said, "hey Joan, I don't know if we tell you this enough, but you're really doing a great job here."

He went on his way, and I swear - I think there were tears in my eyes. And I got back to work, and I felt *really good*. And energized, and happy, and important there, and thank goodness my boss did that for me before I made another mistake, or decided to demote myself. And here's what you're going to do for your people starting today:

Starting today, you're going to express sincere appreciation for an employee. You're going to think of something that person does well, or of some trait that they bring to your company, and you're going to point it out to them and thank them for it.

And really try to make it something unique to them. Maybe someone is especially friendly and welcoming. Maybe someone is cheerful, or positive, or organized, or great at problem-solving, or stays cool under pressure, or is always respectful and supportive to everyone. Notice it (go back to your list on DAY 2 if you need inspiration), and tell them you noticed.

We all want to know that the things we do matter to other people. We want to know *we* matter; that we're special; that we're valued. And we *crave* this at work. When I've asked people what was most important to them at any job, receiving appreciation was an almost constant answer.

This is huge, and you want to use it. So start today, by thanking one of your employees for his/her unique contribution to the company. And the fantastic side-effect, is that the more you do this, the happier *you'll* be. You'll have more energy. You'll feel more fulfilled. And you'll be so grateful for the wonderful people you work with. It's so nice how that works!

Repeat this at least once a week, so at the end of the challenge, everyone who works for you (or at least the ones you come in contact with) will have heard a personalized "thank you!" from you.

day 12 checklist

_____ smile at yourself in the mirror

_____ keep thinking of ways the company *might* support each employee's goals more

_____ do something active

add this if it's a **work day:**

_____ smile at, and greet every person you pass today at work

_____ sincerely thank an employee for his/her unique contribution to the company

day 13

Want to feel like whistling when you walk into work every day? Want to be cheerful, and energized, and much better at handling the situations that suck, and the stuff that hits the fan? Want to genuinely care about everything and everyone there – every day?

Then start putting your personal goals first, and do it first thing in the morning!

These are two lessons I've learned from being a mom:

(1) You will be a thousand times better for everyone if you give something significant to yourself first.

(2) If you don't do it as soon as you wake up (and usually – before anyone else wakes up), people are going to start needing things from you, and the opportunity will slip away with the day.

So let's make a plan for you right now, and make sure you're actively moving in on your own goals. I probably don't need to help you set them, so we'll skip to the part where you're going to give them your time. Tomorrow you're going to get up a little earlier if you need to, and today, you'll set yourself up for success.

(1) Set your alarm now, for whatever time you need to get up.

(2) Plan exactly what you'll do, so there's no time wasted trying to come up with a plan in the morning (which would likely end with you working on work stuff).

(3) Lay out whatever you need for the activity you planned (so if it's working out, lay out your gym clothes and shoes; if it's working on your book, have your laptop, coffee cup, notebook and pen all set out in your workspace; if it's doing research and planning for your non-profit, write a list of the top 3 priorities and set that out with your computer and other supplies).

Repeat this at least 3 times a week for the rest of the time of this challenge.

PERSONAL GOAL TO WORK ON: _____

PLAN FOR TOMORROW: _____

_____

PREPARATION NEEDED: _____

_____

TIME TO WAKE UP AND HOW LONG TO SPEND: _____

_____

day 13 checklist

_____ smile at yourself in the mirror

_____ keep thinking of ways the company *might* support each employee's goals more

_____ do something active

_____ set yourself up to work on a personal goal first thing tomorrow morning

add this if it's a work day:

_____ smile at, and greet every person you pass today at work

day 14

Don't consume negative news today. Even on social media, be purposeful about not clicking on articles about tragedies, crime, politics, etc. If someone you follow consistently posts negative things, unfollow them. Again – we're getting you into a specific mindset about yourself, people, and what's possible, and filling your head with despair is not going to help you.

This does NOT mean you're going to close your eyes to people in need, or pretend that bad things don't happen. There's a difference between looking for people who you can help, or causes you can contribute to, and just seeking out terrible stories to fret over with no other action.

Helping others and making a difference will make you happy. It'll make you feel positive, and reassure you that there's good in the world. Absorbing horrific and tragic stories for information-only will make you feel afraid, angry, depressed, despairing - and you'll probably decide humanity isn't worth saving.

And even things that are meant to divide everyone (*cough* political stories/scandals, debates about social issues *cough*) can be dicey, because if they make you start to feel angry and generalize people, they aren't helping you. Know the difference, and cut things out accordingly. **Avoid negative news for the remainder of this challenge.**

day 14 checklist

_____ smile at yourself in the mirror

_____ keep thinking of ways the company _might_ support each employee's goals more

_____ do something active

_____ work on a personal goal first thing this morning

_____ don't consume negative news

add this if it's a **work day:**

_____ smile at, and greet every person you pass today at work

notes & ideas

week 3

week 3 checklist

here's what you'll do at least 1 time each this week

_____ ask an employee, "how are you?", and then listen to the answer and give a thoughtful response

_____ sincerely thank an employee for his/her unique contribution to the company (you want everyone who works for you – or at least those you can come in contact with – to hear this from you by the end of the challenge)

_____ _____ _____ prepare to work on a personal goal the next morning

_____ _____ _____ work on a personal goal first thing in the morning

day 15

You've been tossing around ideas for how the company *might* help support each employee's goals more, and today you're going to decide whether you came up with anything you can more forward on, and get going if so.

So IF you have a plan for any of the employees, here's what you'll do today:

(1) Write down each plan, for each employee.

(2) Send instructions to anyone (HR, managers, etc.) who will need to put it in place – but see the exception to this in a minute.

(3) Schedule a meeting with the employee, so you can deliver the good news.

And when you do have this meeting, it can be brief, just like the one that got you here. Tell your employee you've been thinking a lot about what he/she told you last time, and that you've had an idea for how to help support the goal. And then explain it.

If you have any reason to wonder whether the employee would want this put in place or not, get his permission or feedback during the meeting, before you set it all in motion. Generally, if it's anything like schedule changes, any unpaid time off, seminars/events requiring travel or occurring during normal days off (even if expenses are covered), major changes to assignments, or anything else you'd want to weigh in on first if the roles were reversed – you'll just want to play it safe and be courteous, and let your employee make the decision or let you know of anything to work around.

And here's something that might have you worried: What if you didn't come up with a plan for every single employee?

Well - I think that's okay. Move forward on the ones you can. I could fill at least seven pages with why we don't all have to be given the same things all the time, but let me try to keep it simple:

Your employees are all individuals with different goals, and there won't be a one-size-fits-all solution, as popular as those are right now.

(But – okay – I just typed that out and I thought of one thing that might be, so that's a couple pages away with your checklist. Just go with me on this for now though.)

Janet might want to be a photographer in the fashion industry, and you might happen to know some people to introduce her to. But those people won't be able to help Barry, who wants to be a helicopter pilot, so for him, you were able to change up his hours to allow for school. And neither of those solutions will help Gina, your receptionist who would love to take a year off and travel. And you might have been able to give her some additional assignments to help her make a little extra for her travel savings, but you might not.

We're all individuals, and your employees are in different positions, and have different situations, and that means the answers for each will be different. I bet you already aren't giving them all the exact same things. They probably don't all make the same amount. They probably don't all have the exact same job description. Or the exact same schedule. When one person takes a vacation, you aren't going to send everyone home. When you give one person a bump up in pay, you probably don't pass out raises to everyone else. When you express your appreciation, you aren't going to use the exact same words for everyone.

This is the same thing.

I know it's scary, because so many of us nowadays have grown up with the practice of "everybody gets the same award for participating", but it's just not like that in life. I mean, of course be considerate, and don't make a big announcement about what you do for each person. They'll probably tell each other, but you won't be rubbing it in people's faces.

If anyone comes back to you and asks why his coworker got something and he didn't, you can explain that you want to be able to help all of them more with their individual goals, and as you come up with ways that the company is able to – you'll do it. Then ask the employee to think about it himself and send you ideas to consider.

I know what I'm saying probably seems to fly in the face of reason these days, and of course this is your decision and you should make it according to what you believe is best. But if you decide to move forward on plans that don't include every single employee, here's a few more pieces of encouragement:

(1) Everything else you're doing during this challenge is going to let everyone know you've got their backs. Everyone is going to know you care and want the best for them.

(2) You can keep thinking about this, and as time goes on, there might be an opportunity to do something for another employee. And maybe later there will be a way to do something for another.

(3) This job is *already* supporting each of your employee's personal goals! What you're doing is just a bonus on top of everything else. Even if you didn't put your plan in place to help everyone support each other's goals, and even if there was nothing you could do to help the company support everyone's goals even more – your employees' positions in this company *already* offer them priceless and relevant skills to learn, traits to develop, connections to make, and opportunities and advantages to take.

That's where I'm leaving you today, but I know you'll be fine. You've got this!

day 15 checklist

_____ smile at yourself in the mirror

_____ keep thinking of ways the company *might* support each employee's goals more, write down any plan you came up with, get it put in place today if appropriate, and schedule a meeting with the employee to discuss

_____ do something active

_____ don't consume negative news

add this if it's a **work day:**

_____ smile at, and greet every person you pass today at work

extra credit

I have a 90-Day Challenge to employees, to help them use their current job to jump-start their achievement of any goal. It's called, *Use Your Job: A 90-Day Challenge*, it's a book like this one, and I'm confident that you'll find it very beneficial to yourself and the company if any of your employees decide to take the challenge. And after everything I just said about how there's not a one-size-fits-all solution for supporting everyone's goals, this might be the closest thing.

If you're still really wanting to do the same thing for everyone, or at least have an option out and available for anyone who wants it, here's where you can get the book:

https://www.amazon.com/author/joanelmore

day 16

Plan for how your position can help you to reach *your* personal goals. It doesn't matter if it's your name on the building; make a plan today for how being in your position in this company can help you to get what you want for your life.

Think about what you want for your lifestyle, health, family, relationships. Think about what you want to have and experience. I'm betting that since you're in the position you're in, you already know how to identify what you want, and set goals, and I'm also betting that achievement of goals is a way of life.

But what I want you to do today, is make direct connections between your work and everything you want to achieve, and have a clear plan for how to make your work give you the things you want.

Let's say you're the CEO of an advertising agency. How will that improve your *health*, and help you to achieve your goal of placing first in a national Jiu Jitsu competition? How can you *make* it help you achieve that goal?

And what about your goal to have strong family relationships by spending quality time every day with your spouse and children – how will your position as CEO of an advertising agency help you to achieve that goal? How can you *make it* help you to achieve it?

How will your role as CEO of an advertising company make you a better person? How will it help you to achieve your goal to help people in impoverished areas to learn business skills and start their own companies? How can you *make it* help you achieve that?

Do that for every one of your major life goals, and think about all the things your position at this company has to offer you that will positively and directly impact your ability to achieve and have those things. Think about the skills your position can teach you; the knowledge it can give you; the character traits it can help you develop; the connections you can make with it; the advantages and opportunities it holds. And plan for how you can take those things and use them to get everything you want for your life.

You know how much you will *love* your company and your place in it, when you're using it to achieve your own goals this way? Again – I'm sure you're already setting and achieving goals as regularly as you eat breakfast in the morning. But what you may not be doing yet is letting your work directly connect to each one of your personal goals.

And what does this have to do with your employees, and how will it impact them and the results they give you?

Well, as I've said before, I'm a mom. And I've learned that all the positive changes and decisions and traits I want for my kids have to come from me first. So take the lead, and enjoy the reward!

day 16 checklist

_____ smile at yourself in the mirror

_____ do something active

_____ don't consume negative news

_____ plan for how your position can help you achieve your own goals

add this if it's a **work day:**

_____ smile at, and greet every person you pass today at work

day 17

I have a four-year-old daughter. And so much of the time, when she's going about the day - eating, brushing her teeth, getting dressed, putting her shoes on, doing a puzzle, braiding her doll's hair – I feel like I need to hover on the sidelines and give her pointers.

"If you hold your fork this way, it'll be easier –"

"Squeeze the tube from the bottom – "

"Ooop – switch those shoes –"

"I think it goes there –"

Stuff like that. I'm not trying to make her feel bad; I just have more experience, you know? I've been through all this before myself; I know the best way to do it. Why not pass along my wisdom at every chance, so she can get maximum results in the least amount of time?

Can you guess today's topic? It begins with the letter "M".

Yep! That's right - micromanaging. It's time to eliminate it, and we're going to start by learning how it hurts you.

I've had plenty of bosses in the past who were a little too clingy. Who would frequently startle me from their silent perch over my shoulder, or interrupt me with a fretful face and an anxious question or piece of advice.

"What are you working on?"

"Why are you doing it that way?"

"How long until you finish this?"

"If you do it this way it'll be faster –"

"Ooop – nope – lemmie squeeze in real quick –"

And these days, I can understand. They were on the line. They were responsible for my results; it would have been really scary to feel like they couldn't control the outcome. But talking about this kind of makes me feel bad for my constant yapping at my daughter. Because every flap behind me and chirp in my ear told me loud and clear: "You don't know what you're doing", "I don't trust you to do this well", and, "You're incompetent."

It killed my confidence. After a while with one boss who had it bad, I was throwing up my hands and calling for him to take over at every turn. I questioned every decision I was about to make and pelted him with questions about the smallest of tasks – even though I knew the correct procedures. It started a distressing cycle where he felt his fears were confirmed, so he hovered even more, and I felt more certain of his complete lack of trust and my own inability, so I gave up even faster. Even at other jobs where the outcome wasn't as extreme, it still made me question my abilities and feel discouraged that my boss so obviously did.

It also derailed my focus. I'd be in the zone, chugging away, and it would all come to a screeching halt as I was flagged down with a panicked question, which was often some variation of, "What's the status of [*a totally different thing*]?" My brain would throw out everything I'd just been doing while I struggled to switch my thoughts and start researching. And by the time I'd looked into whatever-it-was, and reassured my boss that it was finished, or explained the plan for its completion, I'd turn back to what I'd been doing before (*crap - what was I doing?*) and the momentum was too far gone to recover.

Micromanaging is like tying each of your teammate's ankles together before you run a relay race. Your progress will be hindered, you probably won't come out on top, at least one person will faceplant, and everyone will resent you. So let's make sure it doesn't ever need to come from you! We'll get started on your first strategy tomorrow.

day 17 checklist

_____ smile at yourself in the mirror

_____ do something active

_____ don't consume negative news

_____ read both pages of DAY 17

add this if it's a **work day:**

_____ smile at, and greet every person you pass today at work

day 18

You're all ready to make micromanaging a thing of the past – or to not let it begin, if it hasn't – and you're going to start today by giving yourself effective ways to get updates.

You'll set this up, and then – before you ever consider interrupting an employee in person to ask for the status of anything - you'll do two things:

(1) Go to the pre-designated place for getting updates (a shared file, a scheduled report, etc. – we'll get into the specifics in a minute).

(2) Ask for updates with email – instead of face-to-face or with a phone call.

MAKE PLACES TO GET UPDATES ON YOUR OWN

Right now, think about all the projects/assignments/responsibilities you regularly want updates on. If getting those requires you to ask one of your employees, it's time to take that need away.

One company I worked for always had multiple projects going on at the same time, and each project had about thirty major steps that had to be completed by the office. My boss was coming to me at least a few times a day to find out where we were at on different projects, because the information was buried in files/emails/phone calls/programs I worked with, but not in one, user-friendly, easy-to-access place where the status of anything and everything going on could be gotten quickly.

Until we made a spreadsheet. It was my boss's idea, and it saved hours of our time and sanity, and it kept me from launching investigations every time he needed to know if a permit had been filed or warranty information had been sent.

The spreadsheet was in a shared file that everyone in the office could access. It had every current project listed, and then every one of those thirty-ish steps that had to be completed by the office at various points of each project. As a step was completed, whoever did it would quickly go to the spreadsheet and put the date in that step's column. And whenever my boss wondered where we were at in the process of a project, he didn't have to ask.

The answer for you could be something like this; it could be shared files, programs, or systems you all have access to, that can be updated by each person who completes a process. It could be something that automatically updates itself when a process is completed.

Or it could be totally different. You could also schedule regular times to be updated, so you don't have to go asking every time and make it a surprise. If you're going this route, I'd suggest specifying exactly *how* you want to be updated (a report that gets emailed or put on your desk, etc.), *when* you want to be updated (every Monday at 2PM, Wednesdays and Fridays by 4PM, the first of the month, at certain points of a project, etc.), and *what* information needs to be included in the update (P&L's for each current project, sales reports, the status of each active project, etc.).

So do some brainstorming today, and decide what you're going to put in place, so you won't need to go to your employees to get updates.

…As often. And since there's probably not a way to eliminate the need completely, your second plan is:

ASK FOR UPDATES WITH EMAIL

You might not be able to make a system for everything. And even if you do, there might be those times where you need to find out something, and the person who's currently working on it isn't at the point where he/she can type a completion date on a spreadsheet.

So I would suggest at least trying to send emails to employees about this, if you've got any time to spare – instead of interrupting them with an in-person question or a phone call.

And then set up the email for success. In the subject line, put exactly when you need to be updated, and what you need ("Please reply by 3PM today: Has Smith order shipped?" – something like that.). In the body of the email, repeat your subject line and give any more details about what you need.

When you're emailing someone for an update, also be aware and understanding of the possibility that your employee is so engrossed in his/her work that the email goes unseen.

Because of this, when you give your deadline, first make sure it gives you plenty of time to make a second request for the information (in person or by phone this time), for your employee to gather it, and for you to still do everything you needed to with it. And as soon as you send the email, set up an automatic reminder to yourself to go off at the time you'd asked for the update, so you can follow up with your employee if you haven't gotten it by then.

So there's your plan for today:

(1) Set up places to get updates without going to your employees.

(2) Make email your back-up plan.

Do these whether you're a micromanager or not. It will save you and everyone else so much time and make you all way more efficient.

IDEAS FOR GETTING UPDATES: _____

_____

_____

_____

day 18 checklist

_____ smile at yourself in the mirror

_____ do something active

_____ don't consume negative news

_____ make a plan for getting updates without going to your employees

add this if it's a **work day:**

_____ smile at, and greet every person you pass today at work

day 19

We're still on the subject of micromanaging! Yesterday you made a plan for getting updates without having to go to people each time. Start putting that in place today, so it can be followed from now on. That might mean you need to give some instructions to get it going, so do that today.

And now it's time for your next step! This one might take you some time to finish, but you'll start today, and keep at it until it's all set up.

You're going to make sure all your employees have all the resources they need to get their jobs done, with minimal questions, permission, coming-to-ask-for-materials, etc. Even if they don't need to come to *you* for those things, if their managers are consistently getting asked the same questions, or having to authorize things that don't necessarily need it, etc. – you want to set this up to help everyone work better together and get their jobs done more efficiently. Here's how you'll do it:

HAVE WRITTEN PROCEDURES FOR EACH POSITION

Every position will need a procedures manual with clear instructions for every single responsibility that position comes with.

I've been taught that a procedures manual should be detailed enough to teach a person exactly what to do – to the point that they could learn the whole job (in theory, anyway), without anyone explaining it to them (even though it hopefully wouldn't go exactly that way).

And also, that with every procedure, there should be an explanation of what position to go to with questions or for permissions, or to notify about certain things; plus how this task overlaps or supports other positions, and their part of it.

And that with every procedure there would be an explanation of *why* it's done the way it is, so if there's a critical reason (like a company rule or an industry law) not to forge a different path or take a shortcut, there's less of a chance of that happening.

And that a procedures manual should always be digital, so as things change, it can be easily updated, and prevent people from following expired instructions.

Yes – daunting. But you don't have to chain yourself to your desk for the next two years to get this done. Let this be a long-term thing that's consistently being worked on until it's complete, and make a plan for how you can start working on it bit-by-bit. Here's an idea, just to help you brainstorm:

(1) You could make a separate, digital document for each position, and list each of the responsibilities.

(2) Pick a position to start with, and then pick a responsibility, and on the next page of the document for the position, put that responsibility at the top of the page, and then make bullet-points for each major step of that procedure. And also include any important advice/tips/references/laws/requirements/policies that go with it.

(3) Repeat that over time, either prioritizing a certain position (so you can complete one manual at a time), or prioritizing certain responsibilities, so groups of people who work together will each have at least a summary of the correct steps for procedures that overlap. At some point, you'll have documents with bullet-point instructions for each responsibility under each position.

(4) As you go along with this, save the digital files in a place where the employees can access, so they can start referencing the procedures as they get written. And give any permissions and other resources at that time (we'll go over those in the next section), so at least with those tasks, people can work as independently as possible.

(5) After you've got manuals for every position, and they all have those general bullet-point steps and important notes, go back and add details, little-by-little, like before. You can choose topics to tackle as you feel like, or when the right words come to you. And for whatever topic you've chosen, add in the details of the procedure, and why it's done that way.

(6) And in time, you'll be done! You'll continue to refine them, as time goes on, but that part is quick and easy if it's done as soon as a procedure change is decided on.

Yes, it's a lot, but *you* don't have to do all of it! You can delegate this and make it something everyone is working on together. Employees can type up procedures for their own tasks, and those can be reviewed and revised, and then added to over time.

This can be done, and once you've invested in it, it will give back to you endlessly.

GIVE ALL THE PERMISSION YOU CAN - UP FRONT

I used to hate it when I could see the finish line but couldn't cross because I had to wait for my boss to get back to the office and approve something I already knew would be a "yes".

There are really good reasons why certain things need to be approved before people move forward, but sometimes - with the right instructions and parameters – preapproval is the best way to go.

Think about the things your employees have to get your permission to do. Maybe satisfying certain customer requests or complaints. Maybe renewing certain subscriptions or licenses. Or replacing materials. Or choosing between two acceptable ways to complete something.

And then think about how you can empower your employees to make those decisions themselves, as much as possible, and with a happy outcome for them *and* you.

Maybe you could determine a certain dollar amount, and as long as the decision wouldn't cost more than that, the employee could use his/her best judgement and move forward. (And if you did decide to do it this way, maybe have a way to track how many of those costs accrue, so the process can be refined if it ends up needing that.)

Or maybe you can give instructions about acceptable choices in certain situations. Or give other parameters to stay within.

And if you need to make sure it's all going well, you don't have to keep your eyes closed and cross your fingers. You can ask for a quick account of each decision to be sent to you (by email or another quick, digital method, preferably) for the first little bit, until you're comfortable that it's all running smoothly, and the correct systems are in place.

GIVE EVERYONE ALL THE RESOURCES THEY NEED

This might sound obvious, but in almost every job I've had, there was *something* missing; something that was holding me back somehow. Sometimes it was that I didn't have thorough training on a certain task. Sometimes it was a certification, or a subscription, or a program. Or supplies, or a system, or an introduction with someone in another department with responsibilities that overlapped mine.

Brainstorm yourself about this, but don't skip going straight to the source. Choose a way to get feedback from each employee. Depending on the size of your company, you might decide on one mass email (and if that's the case, make sure everyone knows not to hit "Reply

All"). Or you could do this with a survey, or individual emails, or asking each person in person. However you choose to do it, give each employee an opportunity to answer this question:

"What things or resources would help you in your role here?"

Give the answers time to come in, and then consider each one, make a plan, and move forward.

You've got a lot to think about today, but it's going to be *so* worth it. We'll go over the last part tomorrow!

day 19 checklist

_____ smile at yourself in the mirror

_____ do something active

_____ don't consume negative news

_____ plan a way to have written procedures for each responsibility in each position

_____ plan a way to give employees all the up-front permission you can, so they can do their jobs with minimal hurdles

add this if it's a work day:

_____ smile at, and greet every person you pass today at work

_____ move forward on your plan for getting updates without going to your employees

_____ ask each employee what resources would help them in their role

day 20

Last day on the micromanaging topic! And your last step is critical: Communicate your expectations CLEARLY. This is another obvious thing that we all hear constantly, and by now it sounds like something we can tune out. But you don't want to, or you probably won't like the results you're given.

I had a boss who didn't really do this for me, and he was constantly dismayed and frustrated as I got his instructions totally wrong. And then I found myself struggling with the same problem when I was later in a management position.

I've learned for myself – it's hard to do all the time. We're busy; there's a million things to do, and we need this one out of our brain and off our plate, so we can get to everything else. And – you know – sometimes I also didn't want to be too intense about things. I didn't want to seem like I didn't trust people. Or like I was on a power trip. Or becoming a micromanager.

But after years of giving vague instructions and being disappointed, I took a seminar and was told that if anyone missed the mark with something I'd asked for, it was my fault for not communicating my expectations clearly enough. Now I see the light, and the path to happiness, and you can follow it with these steps:

SAY IT WELL

Clearly. With all the necessary details. Remember in school when our teachers taught us how to gather information? "WHO, WHAT, WHEN, WHERE, HOW, WHY" – You want to give all of those, so no one has to guess what you want and hope for the best, and you want to make sure you include a bright and shining description of the **exact results you want**.

And at the same time – you'll want to leave out the excess. I had one boss who would wander through instructions, giving side-stories and inserting her opinion about projects-gone-by, and by the end of it all I couldn't remember what she wanted from me, but dared not ask. So while you're giving a detailed explanation, keep out the unnecessary, so you don't make anyone's ears turn off.

PUT IT IN WRITING

I used to get so annoyed as a teenager whenever I tried to explain to my little brother how to make his own peanut-butter-and-jelly sandwich. I'd start out patiently: Get a plate, put two slices of bread on it, get a knife from the drawer, get the peanut butter from the pantry, get the jelly out of the fridge, spread jelly on one slice of bread, clean the knife, spread peanut butter on the other slice of bread, rinse the knife and put it in the dishwasher, put the two slices of bread together, enjoy the sandwich.

My brother would stare at me with a fretful look on his face, and halfway through my explanation, he'd shake his head in exasperation.

"What? Can't you just do it?"

"No way, it's so simple!" And I'd repeat the whole thing, and watch him flap his hands and whine until I found myself saying everything for the fourth time as I made his sandwich.

He was seven. But no matter how old we get, a lot of us work better with a reference. We can't all get going with no hurdles after listening to instructions. So when you're giving a new assignment, write it down (or put it in an email), with any necessary steps, and the outcome you want.

The people who get a better grasp of things with the written word will thank you, and everyone will have a guide to go back to if they have questions (you know – instead of knocking on your door).

SAY IT WITH A PICTURE

Like the saying goes. You won't always be able to do this (or need to), but wherever you can, give someone an image that will save you from speaking a thousand words.

I had a boss who was great about this. He'd ask me for a spreadsheet, and he'd make a drawing of what he wanted for each column and row. He'd ask me to make a new form, and he'd hand me a sketch of what he had in mind. He'd ask my coworker to design a new brochure, and he'd bring her brochures that had layouts he liked.

You don't have to be an artist, and you don't have to use your own picture, and this most likely won't take away the need to give other spoken or written instructions (or both). But if it can be said with a sketch, diagram, photo, report, or some other example you can come up with – it really is worth quite a lot.

ASK FOR IT TO BE REPEATED – <u>IF NECESSARY</u>

I wouldn't do this if you asked someone to get you coffee, or be at the meeting at one, or to do anything they do on a regular occasion. I wouldn't do this unless it's completely necessary, or you're not going to inspire fantastic feelings.

But when you're giving instructions for something especially-important, and something outside a person's normal scope of work, I'd find a way to have them let you know that you gave them enough to be successful. Maybe something like, "I've got a lot on my mind today; will you tell me how you understood that, so I can make sure I didn't leave anything out?"

Make it natural for you, but try to make this request about *you* possibly not giving your instructions well – not about your employee's ability to understand them.

And that's it! Let's recap the last few days, so we remember the plan:

You're going to give yourself ways to get the updates you need (on your own), you're going to give your employees the resources they need to do their jobs as independently as possible, and you're going to communicate your expectations clearly.

This will all do way more for you than create efficiency, get the results you want the first time, and allow you to hang out in your office instead of behind everyone's heads.

We all want independence. We all crave it, and fight for it, in any way we can. My daughters tell me at least once every hour they're awake: "I want to do it my way!" – and I've learned that it's in my best interest to find ways to let them, as much as possible.

This won't just make people work better because of the organization and efficiency. They'll work better because they'll be happier. They'll have space, and freedom. They'll feel your confidence in them and it'll give them confidence in themselves.

This whole process will take time. And it's going to be great for you.

day 20 checklist

_____ smile at yourself in the mirror

_____ do something active

_____ don't consume negative news

add this if it's a **work day:**

_____ smile at, and greet every person you pass today at work

_____ keep working and moving forward on ways to let your employees do their jobs independently (places for you to get updates, written procedures, authorization, resources)

_____ give instructions and expectations clearly

day 21

Reach out to one person who you feel is a fantastic leader, and ask for advice. You can call, email, message on social media, or set up a lunch, but send your request today.

And when the advice comes, soak it in and take notes.

day 21 checklist

_____ smile at yourself in the mirror

_____ do something active

_____ don't consume negative news

_____ reach out to a fantastic leader and ask for advice

add this if it's a **work day:**

_____ smile at, and greet every person you pass today at work

notes & ideas

week 4

week 4 checklist
here's what you'll do at least 1 time each this week

_____ ask an employee, "how are you?", and then listen to the answer and give a thoughtful response

_____ sincerely thank an employee for his/her unique contribution to the company (you want everyone who works for you – or at least those you can come in contact with – to hear this from you by the end of the challenge)

_____ _____ _____ prepare to work on a personal goal the next morning

_____ _____ _____ work on a personal goal first thing in the morning

day 22

Learn about the people who work for you. Learn about their lives (within reason, of course) and the things that matter to them, so you can care for and show support to them even more.

You're already taking time at least once a week to ask, "how are you?" and really listen to and respond to the answer. **And starting now, whenever you do that, follow up again later to get an update – when it's appropriate.**

So let's say you asked Debbie on Friday how she's doing, and she tells you that she's worried about her mom, who's scheduled to have back surgery on Monday. You listen and give a thoughtful reply, but now you're going to make sure you follow up with Debbie on Monday and tell her you hope everything goes well for her mom today. And then on Tuesday you're going to ask Debbie how her mom is doing.

Or maybe it's Thursday, and you ask Daryl how he's doing, and he tells you he's excited about his son's cross-country race this weekend. You listen and give an enthusiastic reply, but now you're also going to follow up with Daryl on Monday and ask him if he and his son had a great time at the race.

And don't just save this for your once-a-week, purposeful "how are you" – **find all the ways can to learn about your employees and what they care about, and show your support.**

When you do learn something, you can hurry back to your office to jot down some notes if you need to, or set up a reminder to follow up.

Just get to know them, and let them see that you care. Even if you've struggled with this in the past – even if you're so stressed and weighed down with your own life and responsibilities that you normally have a hard time remembering all the names – as you make this a habit, it's going to make your days at work feel so much easier. You'll walk in, see the faces there, and you'll know them. They'll feel like friends. They'll feel like a support to *you*. You'll really care about them, and you'll be so grateful to work with them.

So no matter how much you already do this, starting now, make it purposeful. Get to know your employees, and remember the things that are important to them.

day 22 checklist

_____ smile at yourself in the mirror

_____ do something active

_____ don't consume negative news

add this if it's a **work day:**

_____ smile at, and greet every person you pass today at work

_____ get to know your employees and find ways to show you care about them and the things that are important to them

day 23

Your next strategy is going to give you employees who feel like the success of your company is their personal mission. It sounds like quite a claim, but you'll be testing it out in plenty of ways over the rest of this challenge, and I'm so excited for you to see the results!

To sum it all up – you're going to be asking your employees for their ideas. And you're going to make them all feel fantastic about giving them. You'll start tomorrow, and here's how you'll prepare today:

I wrote a guest blog post, called, "How to have invested employees". Read that today, to give you all the background and get you pumped up, and be ready to start tomorrow. (And yes – you'll recognize some of the details in the article, because we've already used some of them, and now you're ready for more.)

Here's the link:

https://prosky.co/talkingtalent/articles/how-to-have-invested-employees

day 23 checklist

_____ smile at yourself in the mirror

_____ do something active

_____ don't consume negative news

_____ read the article, "How to have invested employees"

add this if it's a **work day:**

_____ smile at, and greet every person you pass today at work

day 24

Think of a challenge, or a problem you're trying to solve for the company, and ask your employees for their ideas.

> "We've consistently gotten lower reviews from customers on [*whatever aspect*] – what do you think might help?"

> "I'm wanting to implement a policy change that will help everyone to do this safer. Will you give me some of your ideas?"

> "I'd like to revise our procedures for this to make it easier for us to complete it faster, with less mistakes, and with less frustrations among ourselves. What do you think we could do differently?"

That sort of thing. You could make an announcement about it, or send an email, or post something in the breakroom for all to see. However you decide to get the word out, make sure you remember yesterday's article, and give your employees plenty of options for submitting their ideas. Maybe designated time during a meeting for those who want to speak up. And the option to email ideas, for those who want credit, but not an audience. And the option to submit ideas anonymously, for those who want their privacy.

Let everyone know when you'd like to get their feedback, and make sure you give them enough time to brainstorm.

Set up an automatic reminder now, to go off when you wanted to have all the responses in, and tomorrow we'll go over what you'll do when that day comes.

Want to know the great bonus that comes along with all this? Besides helping your employees to feel invested in your company, it is such an effective way to make everyone feel trusted and respected. We employees talk about what we think would help the business all the time among ourselves – and most of us assume that management doesn't want to hear about it. We usually figure that the general opinion is something in the area of, *what do the people on the ground really know?*

It will make such a fantastic impression when you want to find out.

day 24 checklist

_____ smile at yourself in the mirror

_____ do something active

_____ don't consume negative news

add this if it's a **work day:**

_____ smile at, and greet every person you pass today at work

_____ think of a challenge/problem you'd like to solve for the company, and ask your employees for their ideas (give plenty of options for submitting)

day 25

Yesterday you came up with a problem/challenge to present to your employees, you requested their ideas, and you're giving them some time to think and get those sent to you.

We're going to start today off with a reminder, to help you to govern yourself with all of this. Because just in case you're eager to please, and eager to include everyone, and all excited to make a giant tasty soup out of every person's idea – let's just establish something before going in:

Your first responsibility is to the people who work for you. Your second is to your company. And – just like with every other case involving the two – they don't have to conflict. You'll just need to use wisdom, and care, and consideration.

You're going to ask your employees for their ideas, and give them (and you) all the benefits of being part of the process of your company's growth and development. …But not every idea will be a good fit. Or a good fit right now. Or a good fit *exactly* as it was proposed. You might not get *any* usable ideas at one time.

It'll be your responsibility to do the sifting, sorting, revising and discarding as necessary. And if you're feeling a little anxious about that, just remember the boss I talked about in the article you read on DAY 23. There's a way to get this right, and that's the way you'll do it.

First – right now – go to your calendar, and open it up to the date that you asked everyone to have their ideas submitted by. Write this page number at the top, so you can come back to this as a reference if you need details.

And today – as soon as you're done reading through the rest of this - make notes on that day in your calendar so you'll remember exactly what to do.

ON THE "DEADLINE" DAY FOR IDEAS:

(1) You'll read every idea thoroughly, thoughtfully, and with an open mind. Again - you do not have to actually *use* it, but think about the positive things you can praise about it, and any ways it *might* be a fit, and see if it makes any lightbulbs start flashing in your brain with something doable.

(2) You'll give yourself time to brainstorm and come up with the solution you're going to put in place. And you'll schedule that time (and set up an automatic reminder, if needed), if you aren't going to do it right then.

(3) You'll make notes of all the specific ways your employees' ideas prompted your own.

(4) You'll schedule a time to follow up with your employees and let them know what you've decided. And on that day in your calendar, you'll write this page number and make notes about the next part.

ON THE DAY TO FOLLOW UP WITH EMPLOYEES:

This part is really important. Even if you're using one of your employee's ideas exactly, you want everyone else to feel included, and you want everyone who participated to feel fantastic about it – whether their idea is getting used or not.

I don't think it matters whether you choose to do this in a meeting with everyone or one-on-one. But what I would try to do – if at all possible – is do this in person. You want each person to see your sincerity, hear your thankful tone, and feel your kind vibes.

(1) Thank everyone enthusiastically for giving their input.

(2) Talk about as many specific ideas as you can (without calling out the person who gave it – just in case they wouldn't want the attention), and share the things you loved about each one. The exception to this is if you're having a one-on-one meeting with each employee, and if that's the case – just talk about that employee's idea.

(3) Tell them your plan. If it's not exactly like any of the input you got, introduce it by saying something like my boss used to: "And you know what you got me thinking – ", or "And you made me realize –", or "And when I was going over your answers, I realized that there were very common themes. We need [*general aspect*], and [*general aspect*], and [*general aspect*] –" Make the wording natural for you, but make it give *them* the credit for this grand plan you're going to introduce.

(4) Talk about things you learned from them (that will help you to be better in your role for them, or that helped you to understand the process from their view, etc.).

(5) Thank them sincerely again.

That was a lot, but you're going to take it all in doable chunks, and you'll be fine. And I'm telling you, it's going to do so much for you!

day 25 checklist

_____ smile at yourself in the mirror

_____ do something active

_____ don't consume negative news

_____ in your calendar, on the date that you gave your employees as the deadline for submitting their ideas, write the page number for DAY 25, plus notes on what to do that day

add this if it's a work day:

_____ smile at, and greet every person you pass today at work

day 26

Listen to something positive, inspirational, or instructional each day, starting today. You don't have to have a quota for the length of time, or the time you do it, and you don't have to tie yourself to a chair or the toilet to get it done.

I do this whenever I can find times during the day where I'm getting other stuff done that doesn't require my concentration. So when I'm making the bed, doing my hair and make-up, making and eating breakfast, doing dishes, doing laundry, cleaning the house, exercising, making dinner, washing my face and covering it in all my bedtime potions.

Instead of listening to music (I do that while I work), or listening to scandals and gossip in the news (I just opt out of that altogether), I search for how to learn some skill I want to have, or how to develop some attribute I want, or just something that makes me feel inspired and good about the world.

You can choose videos, podcasts, or recorded books, and listen while you're washing the car, fixing the car, driving around, walking the dog, painting your living room, unclogging the toilet, hanging out in the bathroom for any reason, sitting in a waiting room, waiting for your wife to come out of a candle store, making your family scrapbook, baking a cake, and any of the other thousands of things we do that we can take advantage of.

I promise, if it feels like a drag at first, it won't for long. You're going to *love* and look forward to this time, and you're going to start looking for every possible second that you can use for this.

And it's going to be so good for you. You'll get so many breakthrough ideas for your company, for your position in it, for your employees, and for your own goals. You're going to become even better for all of those things. And you'll be happier, because progression makes us happy. **So do this every day for the rest of the time of this challenge.**

day 26 checklist

_____ smile at yourself in the mirror

_____ do something active

_____ don't consume negative news

_____ listen to something positive, inspirational or instructional

add this if it's a **work day:**

_____ smile at, and greet every person you pass today at work

day 27

Do random acts of kindness at work today.

If someone is fretting because his kid's game is starting two hours before his shift ends, let him go early. If someone else is having a miserable time with a tedious and mundane task, or doing something demanding and stressful, hop in and help get it done faster. Go clean the bathrooms or the breakroom microwave before someone else has to. Put more paper in the copier. Refill the paper towels. Do all the end-of-day closing procedures. Bring in breakfast, or snacks. Tell everyone that lunch time today is paid. Or that anyone who wants to can leave an hour earlier (and get paid for it).

Like every single other thing that can be taken too far, do this with good judgement, and don't do anything you can't authorize from your position, and don't do anything that will put the business in a bad spot or light a bunch of fires, and don't feel like you have to fill every second of your day with do-gooding and get behind on your work.

Just find ways to be kind to your employees today. And since this will mean so much to them, and give back so much to you – **do this purposefully at least once a week.**

day 27 checklist

_____ smile at yourself in the mirror

_____ do something active

_____ don't consume negative news

_____ listen to something positive, inspirational or instructional

add this if it's a work day:

_____ smile at, and greet every person you pass today at work

_____ do random acts of kindness for your employees

day 28

Set up some DO NOT DISTURB time today, and every work day you possibly can. You can choose the length of time, and the time you do it, and how many times each day you do it, but here are the rules:

(1) You're going to lock yourself away in your office, or leave the office altogether, and unless your grandmother breaks a hip in your living room, or your wife goes into labor, or your husband hits the jackpot on his work trip to Vegas - you won't be available to anyone. All your calls will be held; you won't check your email; you won't even think about peeking at any social media sites; the receptionist will say you're out of the office, in a meeting, or suffering in the bathroom from some bad chicken last night, and no one will come knocking on your door with questions.

(2) You'll use this time to focus on your own work; your biggest priorities that so often get shoved to the back burner the second you walk in the office and get bombarded with everyone else's emergencies.

(3) As soon as the time is up, the receptionist can give you any phone messages, you can look at your email if you want, and if any employees need you, your door will be open.

And here's how you'll put it in place:

(1) Decide when you want to do this, and the length of time, and schedule it into your calendar for those days and times, for the rest of the time of this challenge (set up an automatic reminder for the next couple weeks too, until you make this a habit).

(2) Make a big announcement, explain what you're going to do, when you'll do it, and explain the rules.

(3) Remember what you do in a hotel when you want to sleep until noon without room service coming in, and make a sign for your office door.

(4) Get started, and enjoy the results.

I used to spend eight to ten hours a day in the office, and go home feeling like I hadn't accomplished anything. I used to feel like a frazzled wreck as I jumped to every demand in my inbox, responded to every call, turned around for every "hey, you gotta sec?", and went back-and-forth to the front door for every sales person who walked in.

And one day, I learned about doing this, and I decided that the very first hour-and-a-half of my day would be completely focused and undisturbed. I made the announcement, I shut my door, and I swear I heard angels singing while I actually got real work done.

Want to know what this will do for you (besides making fantastic progress on your biggest priorities)? Your stress levels will plummet as soon as you slap the sign on your door and shut out the world. You won't have that awful nagging feeling that something huge and important is sitting undone while you help someone figure out the problem with his computer, or tell a salesman that you don't need your office supplies automated, or return seventeen calls that can wait.

You'll like everyone you work with even more. Because I have to admit, I got a little resentful for a while, before I made this change. It was my fault that it was all happening the way it was, but in my frustration and immaturity, I sort of forgot that part. I felt like I had at fifteen when I thought the world had it out for me, and it seemed like every person in the building was trying to sabotage my day. After I put this in place, I was happy and excited to see them all again, and I'm betting it will be the same for you.

Your employees will be happier, and work better. You being more cheerful and less stressed will rub off on them, they'll get better at problem-solving on their own (giving them more confidence), and they'll have another way to work with independence. Wins all around!

day 28 checklist

_____ smile at yourself in the mirror

_____ do something active

_____ don't consume negative news

_____ listen to something positive, inspirational or instructional

add this if it's a work day:

_____ smile at, and greet every person you pass today at work

_____ set up some DO NOT DISTURB time for every work day

notes & ideas

week 5

month 2 checklist
here's what you'll do regularly & consistently

_____ help your employees' jobs support their personal goals (*from DAY 8 & DAY 15*)

_____ help your employees support each other's personal goals (*from DAY 9*)

_____ keep DAY 10 in mind while you help your employees to achieve company goals

_____ make your position support your personal goals (*from DAY 16*)

_____ keep working and moving forward on ways to let your employees do their jobs independently (places for you to get updates, written procedures, authorization, resources, giving instructions & expectations clearly – *from DAY 18-20*)

_____ get to know your employees and find ways to show you care about them and the things that are important to them (*from DAY 22*)

week 5 checklist

here's what you'll do at least 1 time each this week

_____ ask an employee, "how are you?", and then listen to the answer, give a thoughtful response, and follow up later (if applicable)

_____ sincerely thank an employee for his/her unique contribution to the company (you want everyone who works for you – or at least those you can come in contact with – to hear this from you by the end of the challenge)

_____ _____ _____ prepare to work on a personal goal the next morning

_____ _____ _____ work on a personal goal first thing in the morning

_____ do random acts of kindness for your employees

day 29

Your employees have hidden talents.

The guy who pays your bills and runs the payroll might be so amazing at storytelling, he could put any crowd in a trance. The lady who answers your phones and takes messages might be so organized, you feel like you're walking into a different office when you get within twenty feet of her desk. The guy taking your clients out to lunch might have so much artistic talent, you'd be tempted to turn the conference room into a gallery on the side.

Someone there is incredibly intuitive, and compassionate. Someone else can keep his head together when something hits the fan and everyone around him loses their minds. Someone there is exceptionally friendly, and inclusive. Someone can bake better than your great-grandmother, or solve puzzles you would sit blinking at, or make music you would listen to all day long.

Your employees have hidden talents, and they would love for those to be recognized here. So your next strategy is to give them the opportunity, and you'll start today by identifying the *other* things your employees are good at, and making a nice big list.

Take the next few days to do the research. Look back through resumes and cover letters; ask around; see what you can find out by observation. Go back to the ideas you were just given by your employees, and see if one of them reveals anything helpful. When you're making small talk with anyone, ask about his/her hobbies.

Make a list of everyone's names, and over the next few days, write down at least one talent for each person.

_____

_____

_____

_____

day 29 checklist

_____ smile at yourself in the mirror

_____ do something active

_____ don't consume negative news

_____ listen to something positive, inspirational or instructional

add this if it's a **work day:**

_____ smile at, and greet every person you pass today at work

_____ have some DO NOT DISTURB time

_____ start finding out and making a list of your employees' other talents

day 30

There's a handy and very valuable skill we all need at work, and today you're going to start practicing it. When I explain the concept, I'm sure it's going to sound familiar. I'm sure it's something you're already doing at least at some level, to be where you are right now. But today you're going to step it all up, and you'll do it with a strategy I call, "being in character."

Being in character is not only a way to be your very best at work (for the entire time you're there); it's also a way to practice priceless skills and character traits you want to develop - and put your development on steroids, because any day at work will give you countless opportunities for practice. Here's how to be in character:

(1) Identify all the skills and attributes you already have when you're at your best.

(2) Identify the specific skills and attributes you want to develop.

(3) Take every item from the lists you made during Steps 1 and 2, and be all of those things every single time you walk into work, and for the entire time you're there.

And those steps might sound familiar. Part of professionalism, really. But you're going to do this very purposefully, and with your employees in mind. You're going to be specific things for them, so that while you're developing yourself, you'll help them to develop too. Here's how you'll do this:

(1) Identify all the skills and attributes you already have when you're at your best.

(2) Identify any specific skills and attributes you want to develop.

(3) INCLUDE THESE: Positive, caring, thankful, understanding, patient, respectful.

(4) Practice being all the things from Steps 1 - 3 every single time you walk into work (or interact with your employees anywhere else), and for the entire time you're there.

And just be prepared – you won't feel these every day. You'll be tired, you'll be stressed, you'll get sick, you'll come in on a day when every single thing has gone to hell, and you'll see certain faces and be annoyed.

Some days you'll feel like if you even crack your lips apart to give a smile, your frustration will cascade out in language your mother would swat you for. Some days you will feel like you absolutely cannot drag out the energy. Some days you'll just know: you CAN'T today. And you'll just be all those good things… anyway. You'll make it a game with yourself, and see how well you can do – even on days when every single one of your buttons gets laid on.

Yes, there will be times for giving feedback, and addressing serious things, so this does not mean you grin like a fool all day, or chuckle while you deliver discipline. But the more you practice a feeling, the more it will become real – no matter how much you already genuinely feel it now. And it'll show through more and more in every interaction with employees. Your attitude (or the practicing of it anyway) will affect your tone, it will affect your expression, it will affect your wording. It will send everyone the right message.

It's okay if your practice feels forced, or unnatural. I know that probably sounds like a shocking crime, with how much everyone gushes about authenticity these days, but I've also heard again and again that *attitude follows behavior*, and I've tested it out for myself and know it's true.

One day you're going to walk into work, see everyone there, and think, "gosh, I've got great people here with me!" And in the meantime, you'll give so much to them just by practicing that feeling. **So do this every single work day for the rest of the time of this challenge.**

day 30 checklist

_____ smile at yourself in the mirror

_____ do something active

_____ don't consume negative news

_____ listen to something positive, inspirational or instructional

add this if it's a **work day:**

_____ smile at, and greet every person you pass today at work

_____ have some DO NOT DISTURB time

_____ keep finding out and listing your employees' other talents (on DAY 29)

_____ be in character at work

day 31

Write down (for yourself) why you love being in your position, at your company, and working with your employees. And then think of someone – anyone – in your life who helped you to get here, and send them a thank-you letter today.

_____

_____

_____

_____

_____

_____

_____

_____

_____

day 31 checklist

_____ smile at yourself in the mirror

_____ do something active

_____ don't consume negative news

_____ listen to something positive, inspirational or instructional

_____ write why you love being in your position and company, with your employees

_____ send a thank-you letter to someone who helped you get to where you're at

add this if it's a **work day:**

_____ smile at, and greet every person you pass today at work

_____ have some DO NOT DISTURB time

_____ be in character

_____ keep finding out and listing your employees' other talents (on DAY 29)

day 32

Since DAY 29 you've been finding out and making a list of your employees' other talents – things they may not get to use a lot (if at all) at work. Today, brainstorm ways you can help each person to show those off to you and his/her coworkers.

It might be through extra or one-time assignments now and then (asking someone who loves writing to contribute to the company's blog, or someone who loves decorating to give the breakroom a makeover, or someone who loves baking to bring something to the next event, or someone artistic to design some marketing materials, or someone who's great at speaking to present during the next meeting).

It might be by asking someone for his/her input or ideas.

It might be with a recommendation to someone else in the company who could use this employee's contribution.

And it might be by letting your employee know you noticed their skill and are impressed.

Think of all the ways you can make each employee feel recognized for his/her other strengths, and all the ways you might help them to use those here.

Then, one employee at a time, put your plan in place until you've given everyone a way to shine by the end of this challenge.

day 32 checklist

_____ smile at yourself in the mirror

_____ do something active

_____ don't consume negative news

_____ listen to something positive, inspirational or instructional

_____ brainstorm ways to help each of your employees to show off their other talents at work, and put the plans in place so everyone gets a chance to shine by the end of the challenge (REFERENCE LISTS MADE ON DAY 29 & DAY 32)

add this if it's a **work day:**

_____ smile at, and greet every person you pass today at work

_____ have some DO NOT DISTURB time

_____ be in character

day 33

I love using email to communicate about work-things at work. I know everybody's sad that we're all buried in screens and losing connection, and that we all need to find out each other's eye colors and say words with our vocals.

But when it comes to the subject of actual work – most requests, assignments, questions, updates, FYI's – I think email is the best way to interrupt someone, because it can be the least interruptive.

Like I've said before, a call, a knock on the door, or a surprise peek over a cubicle wall could make someone completely lose their train of thought and focus, and bring any momentum they had before to a screeching halt. So I love email. ...When it's used well.

And that's why today we're going to go over a few ways you can make sure your employees aren't ever tempted to mark your emails as spam, or leave them ignored for weeks. You'll get what you want, everyone will be productive, and you'll all be happy with each other.

First things first:

GIVE IT A GOOD SUBJECT

Your subject line should completely give away the basic message or request you're going to put into the body of the email. It should completely give away what you need from the person, and when you need them to do it. I know it seems faster to type out, "Please Advise", or "[Project Name]", or to hop over it with a "No Subject", but you never want someone to wonder what your email is about before they open it.

Make your subject lines say things like,

> "Please reply by 3PM today: Has Smith order shipped?"

> "Please email Smith project P&L to me by noon Friday."

> "Please create new job reporting form and submit to me by end-of-day Tuesday."

Yes, they're so long! And you want that. When your employee is busy with something else for you, and sees that you just sent an email, you want him/her to be able to immediately prioritize when to open it, and minimize distraction to the current thing being worked on.

You want your request to be clear, and that will start with the first impression. You'll have a way better chance of getting what you want if your employee's brain doesn't start out by swiping at a foggy subject line.

You also want this email to be easily found and referenced again, if say, it gets read, it gets marked as read, and then it needs to be read again later for a review of the details.

One of my past bosses actually taught me to do this, and he took it a step further by creating a system for subject lines, to make them even more easily prioritized, searched, and referenced. He had a list of key words or phrases to put at the very beginning of the subject line – things like "FYI", "PLEASE REVIEW", "NEED SIGNATURE", "URGENT", and even job-specific things like, "DELIVERY", "PRODUCT ORDER", "PROFIT REPORT", etc. The rest of the subject line followed in the descriptive format we've been talking about, but it also always had one of my boss's key words or phrases.

You can get really organized and start something like that if you want, but the only part you have to do right now is give every single email (or at least the ones you send to your employees) a clear, well-said subject line.

GIVE ALL NEEDED INFO IN THE BODY

Again, you might be in a rush, but you shoot yourself in the leg by being vague.

If you're sitting in a hairdresser's chair, you might not like how it all turns out if the only thing you said was, "make it look good," and she excitedly shows you the surprise design she shaved through the back.

If you're ordering a sandwich, you might not find it mouthwatering if all you gave was, "I like my sandwiches thick," and you're handed two pieces of bread stuffed full of every veggie you can't stand, and drenched in a fiery sauce.

If you're talking to a car salesman, you might end up with buyer's remorse if your only instructions are, "I want something that makes me feel younger," and he convinces you to buy a minivan to remind you of the one Mom used to shuttle you around in.

If you need Accounts Receivable to send you a report of all accounts that have been past-due thirty days, that have not had a payment plan arranged, and are over a certain dollar amount, don't send a hasty, "Need to see past due accounts. No plan. 70+."

Your employee might think you need a list of *every* past-due account, that you have no plan for what to do with them, and that you're either guessing the amount of accounts you'll be sent, or you only want to see accounts owned by people who live in retirement communities.

Remember what we went over on DAY 20 about communicating your expectations clearly, and take the time to give the WHO, WHAT, WHERE, WHEN, WHY, and HOW.

NO UNNECESSARY COPYING

I know, I know – you need everyone to know what's going on, and sweeping them all in with a mass email is such an efficient way to get it done.

But sometimes people who haven't really been part of it all - until now - will get the email and spend way too much time trying to figure out what they're supposed to do with it. They might send side emails (that you aren't part of) and start confusing conversations as they attempt to get a crash course on what it seems like they're "supposed" to be up to speed on. They might even take some other unnecessary action, thinking that they'd better hurry up and get done whatever-it-is that you're wanting from them. And in the end, it can all turn into a mixed-up mess of misunderstandings, and you'll pay everyone for all of it.

The CC is necessary in a lot of cases, I know. And when you use it, add one more minute of time, and let each person you copied in know exactly what they're supposed to do. So you'll have the main message of the email. Everyone is going to read it, and when they get to the bottom of it, they'll see that you typed out their names:

> "KAREN – You'll continue to lead this. Please get with Jim by noon today to get a final invoice for the Smith project, send it to Mr. Smith, and call him to go over it.

> "JIM – Please make a final invoice for the Smith project by noon today, but do not send to Mr. Smith. Give it to Karen so she can send it and go over it with him.

> "EVERYONE ELSE COPIED IN – Read through this email to get familiar with the situation. All calls regarding any aspect of this project should be sent to Karen."

Make sense? It will to everyone else too, and in the end, it will save you time, mistakes, and tons of questions back.

...OR THINKING "FORWARD" SAYS IT ALL

Do you like reading up from an email train that goes back three months, and includes seven people who jump in-and-out and give partial information? Do you really want to invite someone to hop in for the first time, with no other explanation or backstory, and let them move *forward* (get it?) on whatever they think they've learned from the experience?

Yeah, no.

And since forwards are also necessary in so many cases, just add a little extra time to these types of emails too, and make sure the person who gets your "FWD:" is abundantly-clear about what to do with it.

So you should probably summarize the situation. And then explain why you're sending this and exactly what to do. Maybe something like,

> "Mary, these emails are about the Rogers project. As you know, it's been on hold for the past three weeks while we wait for a part to be shipped. These emails are between me and the manufacturer, and I'm being told that they should have the part ready by this coming Tuesday.
>
> "I'm sending this to you, because I'll be out of town for the next several days, and I'll need you to keep following up with the manufacturer to make sure they prioritize this.
>
> "Read these emails to get familiar with what they've been telling me, follow up Friday, Monday, and Tuesday, and direct your calls and emails to Janet (her information is in the emails)."

Yes, it might seem like a hassle. What good is that previously-convenient Forward if it doesn't explain everything for you?

But it'll still quote people. And give a timeline. And give contact information. And it might give a (scattered) story, and some extra details, and an idea of the general mood over the situation. And your little bit of extra time to give it a proper introduction will ensure that it's handled properly.

Let's recap all that. You're going to:

Give your emails a good subject line.

Give all necessary details and information in the body.

Let each person copied in know exactly what to do with the email.

Give a summary and instructions with any Forwards.

That's how you'll send emails to your employees from now until the end of this challenge! And I bet you'll love the results so much, you'll make it a way of life.

day 33 checklist

_____ smile at yourself in the mirror

_____ do something active

_____ don't consume negative news

_____ listen to something positive, inspirational or instructional

add this if it's a **work day:**

_____ smile at, and greet every person you pass today at work

_____ have some DO NOT DISTURB time

_____ be in character

_____ make sure all emails you send to employees have a good subject, all needed info in the body of email, an explanation to each person in a copy, and a summary and instructions with each forward

day 34

Help everyone to be more active at work. Your sales force won't come alive over another box of donuts in the breakroom, and the outbreak of sciatica in the accounting department won't improve with wider chairs to sit in.

Tons of companies do competitions around steps taken in a specific amount of time, and if you want to get in on that, I think it's great. But there are so many more ways to do this, and you can find something that works for you, and your employees.

It might be by encouraging quick breaks every ninety minutes, where everyone stands up to stretch and move around for a few minutes. It might be by having someone come in every month or so and teach a yoga class. Or investing in some areas where people can take turns standing at taller desks, or walking at a treadmill desk, or using some simple exercise equipment in the breakroom.

If your employees job description already involves physical activity, find a way to encourage a different type of activity now and then, to counter any repetitive motions, or quick breaks to stretch.

And no, your place is not a gym (unless it is), and having a bunch of sweaty people congregated for eight hours won't be fun for anyone (unless you own a gym). But I really think that if you take the time to find a suitable method for your company, it'll reward you in so many ways.

I'm willing to bet almost anything that your employee's energy and engagement will increase. I bet they'll all be a lot more cheerful – even on Mondays after lunch. I bet they'll feel more confident. I bet they'll get more work done, and with more accuracy. I bet they'll have less aches and pains, and I bet they might even take a few less sick days. And I'm positive they'll be grateful to you for looking out for their well-being.

All fantastic for you, so do a little brainstorming today and figure out how to put something in place.

day 34 checklist

_____ smile at yourself in the mirror

_____ do something active

_____ don't consume negative news

_____ listen to something positive, inspirational or instructional

_____ think of ways to help your employees be more active at work

add this if it's a **work day:**

_____ smile at, and greet every person you pass today at work

_____ have some DO NOT DISTURB time

_____ be in character

_____ make all emails you send to employees follow DAY 33

day 35

Stop by your employees' work areas to ask how they're doing and if there's anything they need. **Repeat this at least once a week for the rest of the time of this challenge.**

day 35 checklist

_____ smile at yourself in the mirror

_____ do something active

_____ don't consume negative news

_____ listen to something positive, inspirational or instructional

add this if it's a **work day:**

_____ smile at, and greet every person you pass today at work

_____ have some DO NOT DISTURB time

_____ be in character

_____ make all emails you send to employees follow DAY 33

_____ help your employees to be more active at work

_____ visit your employees around work today, and ask how they're doing and if there's anything they need

notes & ideas

week 6

week 6 checklist

here's what you'll do at least 1 time each this week

_____ ask an employee, "how are you?", and then listen to the answer, give a thoughtful response, and follow up later (if applicable)

_____ sincerely thank an employee for his/her unique contribution to the company (you want everyone who works for you – or at least those you can come in contact with – to hear this from you by the end of the challenge)

_____ _____ _____ prepare to work on a personal goal the next morning

_____ _____ _____ work on a personal goal first thing in the morning

_____ do random acts of kindness for your employees

_____ visit your employees around work, and ask how they're doing and if there's anything they need

day 36

At any point today, if someone irritates you, practice controlling your response.

You can feel like snapping sarcastically and speak calmly and respectfully anyway. Your eyes can beg to roll up, and you can point them forward anyway. You can want to throttle someone and keep your arms down. It's part of being in character. It's a skill, and no matter how much you have this mastered, be even more purposeful about it starting today.

You know what my natural reaction is, when someone is fraying my last nerve?

Laughing! But like that bordering-on-hysterical laughing, where the person knows I'm about to snap, and shrilly stutter out how much I can't-freaking-believe they could act this way and drive me closer to insanity. (I have kids.)

Whether you're dealing with an employee or not, and no matter what you feel like doing in the moment, practice with me, and let's get really good at keeping ourselves under our own control. This one is so important for winning the confidence of your employees (and everyone else you work with) and helping them to follow your great example.

Practice this every single day for the rest of the time of the challenge. Do it whether you're working or not, because you want to get as much practice as possible. And I'm confident that people all over will come through for you and provide plenty of opportunities!

day 36 checklist

_____ smile at yourself in the mirror

_____ do something active

_____ don't consume negative news

_____ listen to something positive, inspirational or instructional

_____ whenever someone irritates you, practice controlling your response

add this if it's a work day:

_____ smile at, and greet every person you pass today at work

_____ have some DO NOT DISTURB time

_____ be in character

_____ make all emails you send to employees follow DAY 33

_____ help your employees to be more active at work

day 37

Have I mentioned that I have kids? Maybe a few times.

And there's something I've learned, since I got blasted out of bed the very first night after bringing my oldest daughter home from the hospital:

Taking care of people is exhausting. It's really draining. These days, I can get a full night's sleep and spend all day at home, and still feel like my brain has turned to spaghetti by dinnertime. It's hard to be "on" all day. I'm not constantly in the mood to have an answer ready for a thousand questions, or to make sure my service in the kitchen is satisfactory, or to be available every second to fix a broken dinosaur, or scrub fruit punch out of the grout, or cheer someone through a bowel movement, or get a head unstuck from between the bed rails, or break up a fight over a castle.

And really – it's not so different from taking care of people at work. You have to be your best constantly. You have to be a leader. You have to be the strong one in a disaster. You have to take the brunt of the complaints. You have to take responsibility for everything. You have to figure out how to keep multiple personalities happy. You have to look out for everyone's safety, and their well-being, and their best interest. You have to teach, and guide, and listen, and care, and you probably have your own stuff going on.

So starting today, you're going to do something you love. Something that's just for you, that makes you happy and recharges your batteries. Maybe it's reading a book, or taking a walk, or playing video games, or watching a game on TV, or drawing, or painting, or working on your project car, or baking, or picking up a delicious, already-prepared meal.

And yes, of course, this could be overdone, but I'm not really worried about you knowing where to draw the line. Take some time for *you* every day.

You don't have to do the same thing or do it for the same amount of time, but **every single day for the rest of the time of this challenge, do something nice for yourself, and give yourself something you love.**

I know from experience – you'll be so much happier, so much less stressed, and so much better for everyone!

day 37 checklist

_____ smile at yourself in the mirror

_____ do something active

_____ don't consume negative news

_____ listen to something positive, inspirational or instructional

_____ whenever someone irritates you, practice controlling your response

_____ do something you love

add this if it's a **work day:**

_____ smile at, and greet every person you pass today at work

_____ have some DO NOT DISTURB time

_____ be in character

_____ make all emails you send to employees follow DAY 33

_____ help your employees to be more active at work

day 38

Time to get your employees' ideas again! You can ask this question in person or with email, but make sure it comes directly from you, and that every one of your employees gets it:

"**This is my vision for our company:** [*paint an inspiring picture of the vision*]. **Who do you think we all need to become in order to get to that point?**"

Like before, let them know when you'd like to have all the answers in (let's say a week, if you want to follow this challenge exactly, but you can give more time if you want, and just mark that page to do later), and give several options for submitting those.

day 38 checklist

_____ smile at yourself in the mirror

_____ do something active

_____ don't consume negative news

_____ listen to something positive, inspirational or instructional

_____ whenever someone irritates you, practice controlling your response

_____ do something you love

add this if it's a work day:

_____ smile at, and greet every person you pass today at work

_____ have some DO NOT DISTURB time

_____ be in character

_____ make all emails you send to employees follow DAY 33

_____ help your employees to be more active at work

_____ tell everyone your vision for the company, and ask who you all need to become

day 39

Back on DAY 28, you started giving yourself some uninterrupted time during every work day, and I hope you've been doing summersaults over the results.

Today you're going to share the happiness with your employees, and find ways - for as many of them as you possibly can – to let them enjoy the productivity, creativity, momentum, and satisfaction of focused, uninterrupted time to work.

You might not be able to give all of them the same amount of time, or have them all do this at the same time. They might have to take turns covering the phones for each other, or being available for clients who walk in. You might have to get really creative to find a quiet space for people who are doing this (or start handing out earplugs). You might have to get creative to let everyone else know who can't be disturbed at any given time (if – as is likely - not everyone has their own office to go into).

When this becomes a thing, you'll give them all the rules:

(1) The amount of time they have, and at what time during the day.

(2) During this time, they don't take calls, they don't check email, no one will send them calls, and no one (including you) will come to them with questions or requests.

(3) They'll pick their biggest priority and work on that completely uninterrupted.

(4) When it's their coworker's turn for this, they'll help with calls, clients, and other things that might come up, so their coworker can enjoy the same focused work.

It might take some brainstorming to figure out, like so many other things. But find ways to give this to everyone you can. Iron out the logistics today, and set up a reminder for your next work day, so you'll remember to make the announcement and put it in place.

day 39 checklist

_____ smile at yourself in the mirror

_____ do something active

_____ don't consume negative news

_____ listen to something positive, inspirational or instructional

_____ whenever someone irritates you, practice controlling your response

_____ do something you love

_____ brainstorm ways to give each of your employees uninterrupted time to work

_____ set up an automatic reminder, so that on your next work day, you'll remember to announce and put in place whatever you came up with today (for giving your employees uninterrupted work time)

add this if it's a **work day:**

_____ smile at, and greet every person you pass today at work

_____ have some DO NOT DISTURB time

_____ be in character

_____ make all emails you send to employees follow DAY 33

_____ help your employees to be more active at work

day 40

Learn about how to be a leader instead of a manager. Look for articles, videos, books, podcasts, or ask around for advice. However you want to go about it, do the research today, take notes, and then write down one thing you're going to start doing immediately. **Do that one thing every day for the rest of the time of this challenge.**

day 40 checklist

_____ smile at yourself in the mirror

_____ do something active

_____ don't consume negative news

_____ listen to something positive, inspirational or instructional

_____ whenever someone irritates you, practice controlling your response

_____ do something you love

_____ research how to be a leader instead of a manager, and choose one thing to start doing every day

add this if it's a **work day:**

_____ smile at, and greet every person you pass today at work

_____ give yourself and your employees some DO NOT DISTURB time

_____ be in character

_____ make all emails you send to employees follow DAY 33

_____ help your employees to be more active at work

day 41

You've been making sure to thank your employees regularly, and let them know you notice and appreciate their unique contributions to your company. Recognition matters. We know that already, so you're passing it out.

But there's another way to give this too, and it's just as important as hearing a "thank you!".

Imagine being a kid at the beach. You've just spent an hour building a giant sandcastle, and you're trying to convince your parents to roll off their lounge chairs and come look at it. You're jumping around frantically while Mom puts a bookmark into her novel, and Dad yawns and squints at the sky.

It's so good; it's soooo good!! It'll just take a minute; they won't believe how amazing it is!!

They both finally struggle to their feet and wander behind you to your masterpiece.

You reach the site, and make a crushing discovery. *It's gone.* While you were begging, the tide came up, the castle washed away, and the only trace of your hard work is a small hill where the tallest tower once stood. Even the flag you'd planted at the top is floating out to sea.

Will Dad's, "you can make another," and Mom's, "I'm sure it was wonderful!" be any consolation? Do you think you'll be ready to rebuild with the same amount of enthusiasm?

And how do you apply this to your employees?

Sometimes at work, we can get sent down one path in a project, and put in a ton of time and effort, only to have the scope of work change, or to have the project cancelled, or to have an assignment-switch partway through. And sometimes the expectation is that we switch gears, move on, and keep scrapped work in the past.

It kills our drive.

You can't help it. Things change. You all have to adapt as necessary in order to keep projects – and the business – going. And since that's the case, here's what you'll do:

Take time to recognize the effort your employee made before the whole thing changed. So let's say someone spent the last two weeks on a report, and suddenly you find out it's not needed anymore. Instead of stopping him in his tracks and having him trash it, give him some satisfaction (recognition) for all that work.

Read the report (even if it's not finished), and give him your feedback. Talk to him about what he learned from it; ask him to tell you his process for researching. To make a bigger impact, you could ask him to present it to his team, or even to all his coworkers. Or you could tell him he did such great work that you're going to share it with *your* boss (if that applies - and make sure you actually do). Give him that glow of pride for all his effort, and he'll get going on the next project with even more excitement.

My daughter used to cry and flail around devastated, if I didn't run out to see her tower of blocks before her little sister knocked them all down. She didn't care how much I told her that I could just picture how great it was, and nothing I said could convince her to try to build a second tower. If nobody else got to appreciate it – especially the person she cared most about impressing – it didn't happen. And there was no point in setting herself up for another similar outcome.

Recognition (in every form) matters, so be on the lookout for this additional way to give it.

day 41 checklist

_____ smile at yourself in the mirror

_____ do something active

_____ don't consume negative news

_____ listen to something positive, inspirational or instructional

_____ whenever someone irritates you, practice controlling your response

_____ do something you love

_____ do what you wrote down on DAY 40, to be a leader

add this if it's a **work day:**

_____ smile at, and greet every person you pass today at work

_____ give yourself and your employees some DO NOT DISTURB time

_____ be in character

_____ make all emails you send to employees follow DAY 33

_____ help your employees to be more active at work

_____ start looking for ways to give recognition for assignments/projects

day 42

I learned something really interesting recently, and I think it'll be important for you to keep in mind. You want to find ways to keep everyone motivated, and moving the company along to its goals. And you would think the top way to do that would always be to shower everyone with rewards along the way.

I thought that until not long ago, and now the employee in me feels like a traitor in a way, because I would not have wanted anyone to tell my boss this:

Rewards don't always work.

That's right. It seems crazy, doesn't it? But in fact, there are times when offering a reward for something will actually make people's performance decrease. And on the flipside, there are other times when rewards will increase performance, so you have to know the difference, and navigate this whole thing continuously.

Here's what I learned, and here's how you make your decision in each case:

When work is simple, with very narrow parameters, and no (or at least, very little) **problem-solving required – rewards DO boost performance.** So let's say you're under a time-crunch to get sod down on a huge property, and you want everyone to keep a good pace. Offering a bonus for getting it done on schedule should work in your favor.

When work is challenging; when it requires a lot of thought, and problem-solving – rewards do NOT boost performance. So if you've got people trying to create a better vacuum cleaner, you won't help yourself by telling them they'll get a bonus for inventing it faster than your competitors.

At this point, I really can't say why it's that way, but there are several studies out there to back it up, so I think it's something to consider.

And listen – I'm just the messenger in this case, so take some time today to research this whole subject yourself, and then think about the type of work your employees do, and when offering rewards would be effective vs. not.

But here's some final thoughts, and I stuck them in here because – they might seem to contradict what we just went over.

I have *also* heard a lot of compelling arguments for the fact that *frequent* rewards (especially monetary ones) keep people motivated and performing at higher levels. *And* I have heard about how motivating it is for people to simply receive praise and recognition for their work, as opposed to extra monetary rewards.

At this point you might be throwing your hands up, but maybe just consider how to use all of this together.

Maybe within those challenging projects, there are several steps that are simple in nature, and those might be rewarded with bonuses or other monetary-type perks. Or maybe with the type of work you all usually do, you have an ongoing system of bonuses, but when you're trying to move people along on the occasional challenging assignments, you go heavy on the praise and recognition as a motivator. Or maybe you'll choose certain aspects of a person's work to be paid at a piece rate, and others to be paid by the hour.

I know it; there's a million angles to it all, and so many things to navigate at once, but you can do it!

day 42 checklist

_____ smile at yourself in the mirror

_____ do something active

_____ don't consume negative news

_____ listen to something positive, inspirational or instructional

_____ whenever someone irritates you, practice controlling your response

_____ do something you love

_____ do what you wrote down on DAY 40, to be a leader

_____ read DAY 42, then research when rewards boost performance, and think about how you can apply it to your employees

add this if it's a **work day:**

_____ smile at, and greet every person you pass today at work

_____ give yourself and your employees some DO NOT DISTURB time

_____ be in character

_____ make all emails you send to employees follow DAY 33

_____ help your employees to be more active at work

notes & ideas

week 7

week 7 checklist

here's what you'll do at least 1 time each this week

_____ ask an employee, "how are you?", and then listen to the answer, give a thoughtful response, and follow up later (if applicable)

_____ sincerely thank an employee for his/her unique contribution to the company (you want everyone who works for you – or at least those you can come in contact with – to hear this from you by the end of the challenge)

_____ _____ _____ prepare to work on a personal goal the next morning

_____ _____ _____ work on a personal goal first thing in the morning

_____ do random acts of kindness for your employees

_____ visit your employees around work, and ask how they're doing and if there's anything they need

day 43

Come up with a morning ritual. This will be something you do every single time you flail your way out of the covers, and it'll help you feel awake, alert, and accomplished as soon as you start the day.

You might be an overachiever, and be tempted to make this complicated, but try to make it something easy to stick to consistently.

I have a bare-minimum ritual of some kind of simple exercise – maybe push-ups, or some crunches, or some stretching. No quota at all for the amount of time I spend (it's usually a couple minutes at most), or exactly what I do.

I did that for a while and felt like adding more, so on days where I have more time, I also read something positive, inspirational, or instructional right then (again - with no quota as far as length of time, or number of pages to read).

I do at least the first one of those as soon as I roll out of bed, and it sort of sets the tone for the whole day. So pick your morning ritual, and do it every day from now until the end of this challenge.

_____

_____

_____

_____

_____

_____

day 43 checklist

_____ smile at yourself in the mirror

_____ do something active

_____ don't consume negative news

_____ listen to something positive, inspirational or instructional

_____ whenever someone irritates you, practice controlling your response

_____ do something you love

_____ do what you wrote down on DAY 40, to be a leader

_____ come up with a morning ritual

add this if it's a **work day:**

_____ smile at, and greet every person you pass today at work

_____ give yourself and your employees some DO NOT DISTURB time

_____ be in character

_____ make all emails you send to employees follow DAY 33

_____ help your employees to be more active at work

day 44

Make an employee wellness plan. If your company already has one, study it today, and think of all the ways you can support and improve it.

If you've got people who hunch over their desks all day, encourage them to get up and stretch and walk around every so often. If you've got people on their feet for hours, encourage breaks, and keeping a few different (comfortable) pairs of shoes to change into during work. Encourage people to take their vacation days so they don't burn out.

Give bonuses when people make healthy choices for set periods of time: drinking water instead of sodas at work, getting a gym membership or workout equipment, taking the stairs, getting their annual checkup, getting a flu shot, taking any kind of fitness class, getting massages, taking walks, keeping a gratitude journal, going to the dentist, getting their eyes checked, and eating their veggies.

One of my employers couldn't offer us benefits, but the company started a "health reimbursement", and would pay each employee an extra hundred dollars each month, if the employee provided proof of current health insurance.

Another kept heating pads, ice packs, massagers, and mats for us to stretch out on in the breakroom, and put stocks of feminine supplies in the employee bathrooms.

Like everything else, think about what you *can* do, and do that. And whatever you invest to get it started will be repaid in abundance.

Employee wellness is something I hear again and again whenever that ever-present question of engagement and retention is presented. This is very high on the list of things employees are looking for in a company. When you give it, I think you'll find that every area of your business gets healthier.

day 44 checklist

_____ do your morning ritual

_____ smile at yourself in the mirror

_____ do something active

_____ don't consume negative news

_____ listen to something positive, inspirational or instructional

_____ whenever someone irritates you, practice controlling your response

_____ do something you love

_____ do what you wrote down on DAY 40, to be a leader

_____ make an employee wellness plan

add this if it's a **work day:**

_____ smile at, and greet every person you pass today at work

_____ give yourself and your employees some DO NOT DISTURB time

_____ be in character

_____ make all emails you send to employees follow DAY 33

_____ help your employees to be more active at work

day 45

Look at all the answers you got to the question about who you all need to become to get the company to where you envision it.

Brainstorm ideas about how YOU can become those things, and write them down. Circle the one you're going to get started on first, and **work on that every day for the rest of the time of this challenge.** (You'll get to the part about your employees tomorrow.)

_____

_____

_____

_____

_____

_____

_____

_____

_____

day 45 checklist

_____ do your morning ritual

_____ smile at yourself in the mirror

_____ do something active

_____ don't consume negative news

_____ listen to something positive, inspirational or instructional

_____ whenever someone irritates you, practice controlling your response

_____ do something you love

_____ do what you wrote down on DAY 40, to be a leader

_____ read the answers your employees sent you (about who you all need to become to realize the vision of the company), come up with ideas about how YOU can become those things, and choose one thing to do everyday

add this if it's a **work day:**

_____ smile at, and greet every person you pass today at work

_____ give yourself and your employees some DO NOT DISTURB time

_____ be in character

_____ make all emails you send to employees follow DAY 33

_____ help your employees to be more active at work

day 46

You've got a list from your employees of who you all need to become to realize the vision for the company. And now you're going to help with that process, by making their growth and development your priority.

MAKE A LIST OF SUBJECTS

And don't stop at things related to their job description. Look at what they gave you, and think about the skills and attributes they would need to learn and develop, to become the people they described. Write down all the subjects that come to mind, so you'll have a bunch of great stuff to pick from.

Here's a list I made, to help you get ideas:

Communication	Leadership	Goal Setting
Typing	Writing	Grammar
Time Management	Foreign Language	Increasing Profits
Presenting/Public Speaking	Coding	Resilience
Sales	Writing Contracts	Money Management
Confidence	Listening Skills	Remembering Names
Creativity	Inspiring Others	Charisma
Family Relationships	Being a Friend	Personal Heath/Fitness
Finding/Hiring Talent	Business Development	Entrepreneurship
Being Positive	Mathematics	Customer Service
Collaborating	Reading	Being Respectful
Patience	Acceptance	Being Respected
Tool/Equipment Use	Safety (industry specific)	HR
Organization	Focus	Email/Phone Etiquette
Leading a Meeting	Finance	Homeownership
Social Media Marketing	Test-Taking	Overcoming Objections
Dealing with Difficult People	Area/Industry Laws/Regulations	

PICK A SUBJECT TO START WITH

It might be the same one for everyone, or you might choose different things for different people. Either way, choose the subject(s) to start with and circle/star/highlight.

FIND STUDY MATERIALS

These could be videos, podcasts, books, articles, online courses, seminars, classes, groups, events, guest speakers, and whatever else I've missed. You've got so many free or affordable options, no matter what your budget is. And as you go along with it and continue increasing profits in your business, it will be so worth it to you to invest more into this, as you're able.

Start where you can for now, and find your employees' study materials.

MAKE A PLAN FOR STUDY-TIME

You might decide to have designated times during working hours each week to read/watch/listen to the materials you chose. Or you might pay people their hourly rate or a bonus once they've demonstrated (through a course certificate, presentation, etc.) that they did the studying during off-time.

You might decide to send everyone on a paid field trip once a month, to attend seminars, events, or classes you've chosen.

You might decide on a rotation, so everyone is learning the same thing at the same frequency, but taking it in shifts, so you don't have to shut the whole place down to let everyone learn at the same time.

You might decide to rotate the subjects, or let everyone pick from a few choices. You might have people studying individually, or in groups. You might decide to have them share their progress and insights with each other.

There are so many ways to do this and make it a perfect fit.

Give yourself a week to do all the brainstorming and researching. And then get started. You don't want to put this off when it's something that will do so much for you.

day 46 checklist

_____ do your morning ritual

_____ smile at yourself in the mirror

_____ do something active

_____ don't consume negative news

_____ listen to something positive, inspirational or instructional

_____ whenever someone irritates you, practice controlling your response

_____ do something you love

_____ do what you wrote down on DAY 40, to be a leader, and what you wrote on DAY 45, to become who you need to be to realize the company's vision

_____ make a list of subjects for your employees to study

_____ pick a subject to start with (work on it today, and finish over the next week)

_____ find study materials (work on it today, and finish over the next week)

_____ make a plan for study-time (work on it today, and finish over the next week)

add this if it's a **work day:**

_____ smile at, and greet every person you pass today at work

_____ give yourself and your employees some DO NOT DISTURB time

_____ be in character

_____ make all emails you send to employees follow DAY 33

_____ help your employees to be more active at work

day 47

Over the next week you'll be working on a plan for your employees' development. Today, read the article I wrote on this subject:

https://prosky.co/talkingtalent/articles/how-to-have-the-best-employees-increasing-quality-through-growth

It'll tell you why you want to get this going as soon as possible, and help you get ideas for putting it in place. You'll also see how some of the things you're already doing tie into and support your employees' development, and you'll get a preview of some things to come!

day 47 checklist

_____ do your morning ritual

_____ smile at yourself in the mirror

_____ do something active

_____ don't consume negative news

_____ listen to something positive, inspirational or instructional

_____ whenever someone irritates you, practice controlling your response

_____ do something you love

_____ do what you wrote down on DAY 40, to be a leader, and what you wrote on DAY 45, to become who you need to be to realize the company's vision

_____ work on your plan for your employees' development by picking a subject, finding materials, and making a plan for study-time (finish over the next 6 days)

_____ read online article ("How to have the best employees")

add this if it's a **work day:**

_____ smile at, and greet every person you pass today at work

_____ give yourself and your employees some DO NOT DISTURB time

_____ be in character

_____ make all emails you send to employees follow DAY 33

_____ help your employees to be more active at work

day 48

Reach out to a former employee today! I would do this either with email, or a message on social media, so you can give him/her time to reflect and give you a thought-out answer. You're going to ask two specific questions, and you could do it with a message like this:

"Hi [*Former Employee*],

"You worked with me at [*give some details about when and where, to jog the person's memory*]. This might seem like a weird request, but I'd like to learn how I can be better for my employees.

"Will you please think about your experience there, and answer these two questions?

1. What were my strengths as [*pick one: a boss/a manager/an employer/your specific title*]?

2. What things could I have improved?

"Thank you so much for your time!"

When the reply comes, don't let negative feedback get you defensive or discouraged, and don't let positive feedback make you feel like coasting. Read it all carefully, and use it to keep improving.

day 48 checklist

_____ do your morning ritual

_____ smile at yourself in the mirror

_____ do something active

_____ don't consume negative news

_____ listen to something positive, inspirational or instructional

_____ whenever someone irritates you, practice controlling your response

_____ do something you love

_____ do what you wrote down on DAY 40, to be a leader, and what you wrote on DAY 45, to become who you need to be to realize the company's vision

_____ work on your plan for your employees' development by picking a subject, finding materials, and making a plan for study-time (finish over the next 5 days)

_____ reach out to a former employee

add this if it's a **work day:**

_____ smile at, and greet every person you pass today at work

_____ give yourself and your employees some DO NOT DISTURB time

_____ be in character

_____ make all emails you send to employees follow DAY 33

_____ help your employees to be more active at work

day 49

Write a letter today. This will be an actual hand-written letter that you'll stick in an envelope, attach a stamp to, and put into the mailbox.

The letter will be to one of your employees, and in it you'll express specific things this employee has done well, his/her strengths, and things you admire about his/her character.

You'll end it by telling this employee how much it means to you that he/she is part of the company, and you'll give a heartfelt "thank you".

Write and mail out at least one of these letters today, and if you have time for more, that's great! **Just make sure to take time at least once a week to send out some more letters, so that by the end of this challenge each of your employees will have received one of these from you.**

day 49 checklist

_____ do your morning ritual

_____ smile at yourself in the mirror

_____ do something active

_____ don't consume negative news

_____ listen to something positive, inspirational or instructional

_____ whenever someone irritates you, practice controlling your response

_____ do something you love

_____ do what you wrote down on DAY 40, to be a leader, and what you wrote on DAY 45, to become who you need to be to realize the company's vision

_____ work on your plan for your employees' development by picking a subject, finding materials, and making a plan for study-time (finish over the next 4 days)

_____ write and send a letter to a current employee

add this if it's a **work day:**

_____ smile at, and greet every person you pass today at work

_____ give yourself and your employees some DO NOT DISTURB time

_____ be in character

_____ make all emails you send to employees follow DAY 33

_____ help your employees to be more active at work

_____ give your employees some DO NOT DISTURB time (to focus on work)

notes & ideas

week 8

week 8 checklist

here's what you'll do at least 1 time each this week

_____ ask an employee, "how are you?", and then listen to the answer, give a thoughtful response, and follow up later (if applicable)

_____ sincerely thank an employee for his/her unique contribution to the company (you want everyone who works for you – or at least those you can come in contact with – to hear this from you by the end of the challenge)

_____ _____ _____ prepare to work on a personal goal the next morning

_____ _____ _____ work on a personal goal first thing in the morning

_____ do random acts of kindness for your employees

_____ visit your employees around work, and ask how they're doing and if there's anything they need

_____ write and mail a letter to an employee, thanking him/her for being part of the company, expressing specific things he/she has done well, his/her strengths, and things you admire about the employee's character (write enough of these each week so that all employees have received one from you by the end of the challenge)

day 50

There's a saying I've gotten hammered with from the moment I started spreading the joyous news that I was expecting my first little bundle:

"Consistency is key."

I could ignore it when I was pregnant, but once a new person was living in our house, I began to understand. I couldn't say bedtime was at eight o'clock and then let my daughter stay up until ten. I couldn't tell her that if she kept up her tantrum we were leaving the store, and then continue reading cereal boxes while she wailed. I couldn't give her a cupcake with dinner one night and expect her to wait for it until after her peas the next.

I had to set the parameters, and the expectations, and the general routine of things… and I had to stick with them. And if I didn't stick with them, she wouldn't respect them, or trust them - or me. So let's just touch on the subject of consistency today, so you can make sure it's being remembered and stuck to. Consistently.

Because policies, procedures, priorities, plans, goals, and ideas that change with the wind will drive everyone crazy. And when the constant changes come from people in management, employees will experience frustration and stress, and will lose respect for the company at every level.

This probably does not seem like something that would be a problem. It seems so basic and obvious, but that's what I thought too before I started sharing my room with a newborn. And when I think back to the places I've worked, I have examples from all of them where inconsistency led to a mess of one kind or another.

At one job, I was taught by a manager to follow up with clients a certain way. I did that for weeks, and then my employer found out and got upset that I wasn't doing it in a way he would prefer.

At another, the policy manual stated that vacation time would be paid out a certain way. My coworker took some days off, and requested his vacation pay the way it was stated in the manual. But our boss thought the policy was something else, and my coworker's check was not what he expected.

And at another, a procedure for reporting certain information was changed, but notice of the change didn't come until months later, in a memo that announced a widespread disregard to the new procedure, and promised disciplinary action for continued failure to comply.

This is something you'll really have to stay on top of. You'll need to make sure that things happen the way employees were made to expect they would happen. The methods, the rewards, the consequences – they all have to be able to be relied upon.

This does *not* mean you can't make changes. You'll just need to make sure they're made in an organized way. Following whatever procedures or parameters you've already established. And that changes are communicated clearly to everyone, and that all the resources needed to navigate the change successfully are given to everyone.

And just a heads up - people in management positions may struggle with this whole thing. Sometimes the higher someone's position, the more out-of-touch they get with the details. This might be a challenge for you too, but you're going to need to do everything you can to protect yourself, your managers, and everyone else from a scenario where a statement is made and not taken seriously, or a riot is caused by seeming wishy-washy, or employee trust is lost with regular contradictions.

Make sure you (and everyone else your employees report to) remember that phrase I've had to keep in mind as a mom: "Consistency is key".

day 50 checklist

_____ do your morning ritual

_____ smile at yourself in the mirror

_____ do something active

_____ don't consume negative news

_____ listen to something positive, inspirational or instructional

_____ whenever someone irritates you, practice controlling your response

_____ do something you love

_____ do what you wrote down on DAY 40, to be a leader, and what you wrote on DAY 45, to become who you need to be to realize the company's vision

_____ work on your plan for your employees' development by picking a subject, finding materials, and making a plan for study-time (finish over the next 3 days)

add this if it's a work day:

_____ smile at, and greet every person you pass today at work

_____ give yourself and your employees some DO NOT DISTURB time

_____ be in character

_____ make all emails you send to employees follow DAY 33

_____ help your employees to be more active at work

_____ be consistent (and make sure management is too)

day 51

Know what to do about low-performers. I know the whole point of this challenge is to have a place full of the very best, but the reality is that no matter how wonderfully-wonderful you make yourself as a leader, and how out-of-this-world-fantastic the work environment is for your employees, you're going to have a person now and then who isn't really meeting your expectations.

And since that's the case, let's go over your strategy today, so when the day comes (or if it's already here), you won't have to waste any time wringing your hands or making the problem worse. There's a short answer to this whole thing, and we'll start with that:

When you've got low-performing employees, you'll need to either make them better, or... let them go. Those are your choices, and they won't be that simple when you're following through on them.

So let's talk about this by making two very broad generalizations and dumping a bunch of people in: (1) people who have performance problems because of a lack of knowledge or skills, and (2) people who have performance problems because of attitude and/or non-compliance to policies or procedures.

GROUP 1: LACK OF KNOWLEDGE/SKILL

You're going to work your face off to help these guys, so let's talk about them first. These are people who are dependable. They say they'll be somewhere, and they show up on time, every time. They say they'll do something, and they do it, on time. They're honest. They're kind. They work well with others. They work hard; they really try to do well. They have a great attitude. You trust them to do the right thing. ...It's just that you keep getting disappointed by the quality of their work. *(Keep in mind, we're generalizing here; go with me on this for now.)*

This might just be my opinion, but I personally feel like all those wonderful character traits I listed off are a lot harder to find and to teach than a technical skill. Yes, this person could have been screened a little more during the hiring process, to make sure he/she also had the skills or experience needed, but it's done now, they're here, and at this point I'd really try to hang on to an employee who demonstrated exceptional personal attributes. Plus – your job now is to look out for your employees; to support them, to have their backs, and to give them what they need to succeed. I'd keep those things at the front of my mind if I was dealing with an employee from the first group, and that would make me do everything I could to help him/her.

Let me just toss out some ideas, and they aren't in a particular order:

Additional training, in whatever skill it is (whether that's communication, product knowledge, sales, confidence, problem-solving, tool/equipment use, typing, phone etiquette, mathematics, your company's particular methods/procedures, etc., etc., etc.). This is probably the most obvious one, and there are a million ways to give it, and we already talked about a bunch of them on DAY 46.

Different responsibilities. If the training doesn't work, I'd try this. And I'd skip straight to this, if it seemed like the employee just wasn't really thriving in the current position. Sometimes it's just that someone is a square peg in a round hole, and if you find a new area that uses their strengths, it'll be like the time you put your wilting plant into a new pot in the sunshine and watched it blossom.

Having a heart-to-heart. Sit down for a talk, but not one where you come in to lecture. Walk into it with concern, and care for your employee, like you would a friend going through a hard time. Go into it wanting to learn how you can help. And then ask. Maybe with something like, "I appreciate you so much; I want to make sure I'm doing everything I can to help you thrive here. Is everything okay? Is there something I can do to help?"

You never know what's going on in someone's personal life; what pressures or hardships they might face, or what experiences have made them the way they are. Or what's going on at work that you haven't seen. Give them a safe place to help you understand, and then you can both come up with a solution together. And in a lot of cases, just feeling heard and cared for can give someone the courage to make changes on their own.

Some help with prioritizing or organizing responsibilities. Certain positions get a lot thrown at them. I've been in positions where I was told my responsibilities were one thing, but then I was also shoveled over everything else that no one wanted to do. I was expected to get my core responsibilities done on time, while also being able to drop that work at a second's notice, and take care of nine other things that various other people would give me. Everything seemed just as urgent, and in the overwhelm, I'd unconsciously sacrifice quality for the sake of getting it all done in time.

If there's any chance that your employee could be in this position, it's time to delegate things to other people, or allow more time to get things done. It would also be critical to help your employee to understand which responsibilities come before everything else, so he/she can confidently move forward on them without wasting twenty minutes in angst every time a new task is thrown on the desk. And if you could possibly give some guaranteed time every day for working with zero interruptions (like we went over on DAY 39), that would probably end up being fantastic for both of you.

Some relief from burnout. Even if your employee seems fine, and his/her responsibilities don't seem overwhelming, you never know what other things are going on that could be causing the candle to burn at both ends. You might need to have a talk to find that out, but you might also get clues from observing. If your employee has been taking work home, or dashes straight from your parking lot to a second job, or you hear about someone caring for an ailing parent – chances are, if the quality of that person's work is suffering, burnout could be the cause.

And in that case, it's probably time for you to step in and offer some R&R. You might have to get creative, or generous, in case your employee can't afford a bunch of days off with no pay. But even some less-intense assignments for a while, or leaving an hour or two earlier each day (with full pay), or encouragement from you to use those paid vacation days, could go a long way.

So would acknowledgement. I know at the times I've felt spread tissue-thin, I had this secret longing for someone to say, "hey I've noticed you're working really hard and I appreciate it. Are you alright though? Do you need a break?" Gosh, just typing the words makes my mouth water. Your employee would love this too.

All the resources needed to do the job successfully. This goes back to what we went over on DAY 19, so go back to that part of the book and think about whether giving written procedures, or certain permissions, or other tools or resources would set your employee up for success.

An environment/management style best-suited to them. This one might be tough to admit, but it's just a fact: not everyone flourishes from all the same factors. It's why parents of multiple children will tell you that they have to adjust their parenting style for each kid's personality. It's why I didn't give my dog a litter box and ball of yarn, and it's why my palm tree turns brown when I start treating it like my orchid.

I know a business owner who hired a golden find, from the looks of things. This new employee was smart, driven, kind, eager to learn, excited about the position, and had experience in a similar position where he'd done really well. He started out in his new job, and everyone was optimistic.

…But sometime around the end of Month Two, his boss was frustrated. He just wasn't seeing any results. And the employee was frustrated. He struggled to do what was expected of him, but he couldn't seem to find his groove. This employee and his employer parted ways after less than a year, both feeling let down.

What happened? How did this employee who came so qualified, and with such high recommendations, suddenly do a one-eighty? Is it because he just decided to stop trying? I was confused about it myself, until I did a little digging.

Turns out, this employee also had a background in the military, where he'd excelled. And I've never been in the military, but I've got enough of an understanding to know at least part of why it was the right fit: The (now-former) employee was meticulous, organized, and extremely by-the-book. At his first civilian job – where he also excelled - he worked for a company with strict procedures, tight parameters, clear instructions, and regular feedback.

This new job (the one that ended so badly) was at a small company. Things were a little unorganized. People wore multiple hats. New employees were given minimal instructions before being thrown into their roles without floaties, policies and procedures were inconsistent, and people in management positions were so busy trying to stay on top of everything that feedback was rare.

And I can't help but wonder now, if it all could have turned out differently. But at least you can use this example, and see if it might apply to someone in your place.

Those are my ideas for the first group, but I'm sure there are even more things you can try, and I'd *highly* encourage you to research this more and see what's worked for other people. Like I said before, you really want to do everything you can to help this first group do well, and make letting them go your last resort.

…AND – still have the courage and good judgement to let them go when it's necessary – whether that's six months from now or next week. Only you will be able to answer that, but you've got to for the sake of your business, and everyone else who depend on its success.

*If the day comes that you know you've really tried and it's still not working out, and you've got to have that talk with a person who has also really tried, and who is everything you want character-wise, I'd do whatever I could to make the transition to a new job as painless as possible.

A glowing letter of recommendation. A connection with a business owner you know, with a company that might be a better fit. A couple weeks or even a month of pay, while he/she is out job hunting (you'd spend more than that keeping an employee on who isn't going to give you the results you need).

For the really good ones, I'd keep trying to help them even as they departed. I'd want that reputation, and karma, and stretch for myself.

GROUP 2: "BAD ATTITUDE" AND/OR NON-COMPLIANCE

First off, let's remind ourselves that we have no way of knowing everything these employees are facing in their personal lives, or everything they've faced in the past, or how they've been treated, or how they feel about themselves.

We don't know what they go home to, who they go home to, what is said to them, what has been said to them, what is said about them, what is said about the things that are important to them, or what the people they care about believe about them, or what they believe about themselves. We just don't know, and we won't fully - no matter how hard we try to learn.

Let's just remember that and have a ton of compassion, so when our frustration tempts us to label them as "lazy", or "rude", or "selfish", or "entitled", or whatever-else – we'll be able to quiet that down.

But you also don't want to keep them around once it becomes apparent that they aren't going to get better here, and you'll need to figure that out fast.

Here's my thoughts on your strategy:

> **Start with a heart-to-heart.** Just start here. And make sure to keep your attitude completely compassionate and kind, and assume walking into it that your employee is a good person who's going through a rough time. You could say something like, "Hey I've noticed that [*whatever thing - name the behavior without putting labels on the person*] has been happening. Are you okay? What's going on?"

> You'll hopefully start a great conversation, where you and your employee both

understand each other better, and in the best-case scenario, showing your employee how much you care will inspire a change of ways. But – this might not be the case every time, so:

Based on whatever you find out, make a plan. That might include things you agreed on with your employee during your conversation, or it might be decisions you make alone, but it might include things like a probationary period, or a mentor, or anything from the list we already made for the first group (and I would recommend that you do try things from that list).

Test out your plan for a designated time, but don't wait too long. Figure out as soon as possible whether your employee has seen the light and is walking the straight-and-narrow.

If the sad truth is that your efforts didn't help the situation, my opinion is that it's time to cut the cord and let your employee go (following your company's specific procedures for that). And now I have to make a big disclaimer, because I said that without any idea about whether you can actually make that decision yourself. I don't know your area laws, industry laws, company policies, or any specifics about your situation, so I'm standing at my kitchen counter like your nosy aunt without a clue. This might not be possible in your situation, and if that's the case, go back to all those things you'd try for an employee in the first group, and work like crazy to help your employee to become better.

Because now it's time to talk about what <u>DOESN'T WORK</u>:

MIXING A LOW-PERFORMER WITH HIGH-PERFORMERS

This is one case where you don't want to celebrate differences and mix everyone up, or even throw in one wild card. You would think that one low performer, tossed in with a bunch of superstars, would be influenced to rise to the occasion and improve. But there are lots of studies out there suggesting that this scenario has the opposite effect, and drags down the whole group.

You'll have to be really careful about the people you put together - and the people you allow to stay in the company – because one bad apple really can spoil the whole bunch.

TRYING TO DISAPPOINT/DISCOURAGE YOUR EMPLOYEE INTO QUITTING

This is a common decision made out of desperation, and it usually goes something like this:

The employer is uncomfortable about the potential conflict, or afraid of legal or other backlash, and so instead of addressing the issue head-on, the thought is that maybe the employee can be influenced to jump ship without having to be fired or sat down for an unhappy talk.

So he/she is given work that no one else wants to do, or held back from promotions or raises without a clear explanation, and is denied bonuses or other privileges, all while being given vague reasons for these things.

And please don't misunderstand me – I do not think you need to give someone rewards when they aren't doing what they need to do to earn them, and I completely agree that your company's policies about disciplinary action must be followed. I'm talking about the cases where the consequences are given, but the real reason for them isn't communicated to the employee.

And I'm talking about the cases where you have every legal right to let an employee go, every one of your company/industry/area requirements for doing that is met, your employee has demonstrated clearly that there's no change on the horizon, and you avoid showing him/her the door because it's going to be an uncomfortable conversation, or you don't want to pay out for an unemployment claim, and so you decide to discipline indefinitely until the employee is finally exasperated enough to hand you that blessed resignation letter.

I hope this makes sense, because there are grey areas, and exceptions, and ways to misunderstand anything. This is going to take so much careful thought and good judgement on your part. The point of this point I'm making is just this:

If you make discouragement into quitting your strategy, the employee might finally walk, but probably not before doing a lot of damage and making a bunch of noise.

I personally believe that discouragement is your enemy, and you want to keep it away from everyone as much as you can. Because whether it results in an employee who sets his speed at idle, or spreads complaints and pessimism through the halls, it's going to hurt you.

THINKING YOU'RE TOO BUSY TO LOSE THE MANPOWER

Having bodies in the building doesn't help you if they aren't working well. You will spend *so* much more time putting out fires, fixing mistakes, and talking people down from the brink or a battle if you keep even one person on who should be gone, or leave one person to keep floundering because you're too busy to help him/her get better.

And all of that will be *so costly* – in actual dollars. I want to put some crying faces here, and draw a picture of a pile of money in flames, but instead, I'll just hope that everything I've gone on about is sinking in and making you nod your head.

THINKING YOU'LL MAKE A NEGATIVE IMPACT ON MORALE BY FIRING

You owe your employees good people to work with. You owe them people who encourage them, support them, and help them to become better. And you'll only give everyone that, if everyone is offering those things to each other.

Keep in mind what I said about mixing high and low-performers: you won't like the outcome, and neither will your other employees. I've seen this tried in so many companies, and all it did was frustrate the great employees, and bring morale and output down.

You want to think of your company as an exclusive club. Remember that from the intro? You want to have a place that only the best people can be part of, because once they're here, you're going to take care of them. And if someone happens to get in and doesn't live up to the expectations after being given all the available help, they must be quickly escorted from the club. You owe that to the other members.

As long as you are truly giving your best for your employees, and looking out for their well-being, and giving them the things we've been going over and putting in place through this challenge, I'm confident that your ability to make the tough decision when it's necessary will actually increase morale.

That was a ton. I know. And it isn't all obvious, or easy to navigate. People can be a combination of things, and at different levels. You might be a small business, and that will make this whole thing a bigger challenge. You might have less manpower, less resources, less available positions, less room for compromises, less time to give.

It will never be simple. But there's the start of your plan anyway, and all the effort is part of what you signed up for the second you made your first hire. You can do this!

day 51 checklist

_____ do your morning ritual

_____ smile at yourself in the mirror

_____ do something active

_____ don't consume negative news

_____ listen to something positive, inspirational or instructional

_____ whenever someone irritates you, practice controlling your response

_____ do something you love

_____ do what you wrote down on DAY 40, to be a leader, and what you wrote on DAY 45, to become who you need to be to realize the company's vision

_____ work on your plan for your employees' development by picking a subject, finding materials, and making a plan for study-time (finish over the next 2 days)

_____ know what to do about low-performers

add this if it's a **work day:**

_____ smile at, and greet every person you pass today at work

_____ give yourself and your employees some DO NOT DISTURB time

_____ be in character

_____ make all emails you send to employees follow DAY 33

_____ help your employees to be more active at work

day 52

You've spent the last five days working on a plan for your employees' development, and tomorrow you're going to put that plan in place.

Spend today ironing out the last details and preparing for tomorrow. If you need to reference what we went over when we started this process, it was on DAY 46.

day 52 checklist

_____ do your morning ritual

_____ smile at yourself in the mirror

_____ do something active

_____ don't consume negative news

_____ listen to something positive, inspirational or instructional

_____ whenever someone irritates you, practice controlling your response

_____ do something you love

_____ do what you wrote down on DAY 40, to be a leader, and what you wrote on DAY 45, to become who you need to be to realize the company's vision

_____ work on your plan for your employees' development by picking a subject, finding materials, and making a plan for study-time (finish today)

add this if it's a **work day:**

_____ smile at, and greet every person you pass today at work

_____ give yourself and your employees some DO NOT DISTURB time

_____ be in character

_____ make all emails you send to employees follow DAY 33

_____ help your employees to be more active at work

day 53

Put your employee development plan in place today, and remember the phrase we talked about on DAY 50: Consistency will be key with this (just like so many other things)!

day 53 checklist

_____ do your morning ritual

_____ smile at yourself in the mirror

_____ do something active

_____ don't consume negative news

_____ listen to something positive, inspirational or instructional

_____ whenever someone irritates you, practice controlling your response

_____ do something you love

_____ do what you wrote down on DAY 40, to be a leader, and what you wrote on DAY 45, to become who you need to be to realize the company's vision

add this if it's a **work day:**

_____ smile at, and greet every person you pass today at work

_____ give yourself and your employees some DO NOT DISTURB time

_____ be in character

_____ make all emails you send to employees follow DAY 33

_____ help your employees to be more active at work

_____ put your employee development plan in place

day 54

This one will be scary, but close your eyes and take the plunge. Ask everyone to submit their answers to this anonymously: **"What would make me a better** [*your position/title*] **for you?"**. Give everyone a week to submit their answers, and understand the rules now:

NO freaking out, getting discouraged, or getting mad about criticism. NO allowing your head to swell and your chair to tip back over anything positive. And NO avoiding the question out of fear.

Asking this will already make you look really good, responding well to it will do even more, and getting the answers straight from the source will be golden.

day 54 checklist

_____ do your morning ritual

_____ smile at yourself in the mirror

_____ do something active

_____ don't consume negative news

_____ listen to something positive, inspirational or instructional

_____ whenever someone irritates you, practice controlling your response

_____ do something you love

_____ do what you wrote down on DAY 40, to be a leader, and what you wrote on DAY 45, to become who you need to be to realize the company's vision

add this if it's a work day:

_____ smile at, and greet every person you pass today at work

_____ give yourself and your employees some DO NOT DISTURB time

_____ be in character

_____ make all emails you send to employees follow DAY 33

_____ help your employees to be more active at work

_____ ask your employees to submit their answers to this question: "What would make me a better [*your position/title*] for you?"

day 55

If tomorrow morning as I'm heading to my car, an eagle soars overhead and times its droppings perfectly, and I'm late to an appointment because I had to get back in the shower – was that potentially a situation where I was spared something worse, or was it just something that happens?

Personally, I really don't know. I am pretty confident that in the moment I'd offend my neighbors by exploding a recital of every bad word I've ever heard of, and I'm sure I'd storm and curse my way through cleaning up and getting back to my car, and I can imagine that I'd repeatedly ask the sky why the **** this had to happen to me today.

But I *hope* that after I'd recovered and come back to my senses, I would tell myself something like, "well – maybe I would've rear-ended someone if I'd left at that time." Or, "maybe I would've gotten a speeding ticket," or "thank goodness that bird wasn't flying over me in the parking lot!"

I value optimism, see. I believe in positivity.

And today I'm going to push it on you, because I believe having it is in your best interest. Remember on DAY 30 when we went over the idea of "being in character," and all those great things you're going to be – and practice being – every time you're at work? Being positive was one of them, so you're hopefully already being/practicing it.

I just have to give it a little more time today though, because I think positivity gets a bad rap sometimes. It seems to be easily-misunderstood – by people on both sides of it.

I've been told at least ninety times that optimism sinks a ship, and that people possessing it are the first to perish in a disaster, so let's start out by talking about what you're NOT going to do with all this:

You're NOT going to close your eyes in hope. You're NOT going to start wishing problems away. You're NOT going to chant happy outcomes and wait for the universe to deliver you to safety. You're also NOT going to become unbearable by countering every grumble with an instruction to breathe and believe.

…But you also are NOT going to tune out the possibilities. And you are NOT going to cower in fear. And you are NOT going to throw your hands up and decide it's hopeless.

You're going to believe that there's a way through anything. You'll be able to see the obstacles, and realize difficulty, and anticipate challenges, and admit that the first way you try might not go according to plan. But you'll believe that there is a way. It'll be a puzzle you can solve; something with an answer you know you can find if you don't give up. And you'll communicate that to your employees on the days when everything has hit the fan, and everybody will feel a little braver.

And you're going to believe in the goodness of people. No matter how many times you've been let down, or shown the worst, or given reason to think otherwise, you'll believe that there is always more good than bad; that most people really are kind, and trying their best, and looking out for each other. And believing that will influence the way you see and interact with your employees.

And you're going to believe in all the opportunity in the world. It'll inspire you, and give you ideas, and help you to recognize and use advantages. It'll keep you going when one thing doesn't work, and someone tells you they aren't interested, and someone else gets there first. The world is full of opportunity, so you can keep going for as long as it takes, and you'll help your employees to do the same.

That's how you'll be positive. And you might not believe any of that stuff in your personal life, and that's okay. You'll be in character at work, so you can *practice* whenever you're there. And I promise – it'll give you the courage you need, and it'll give it to your employees, and you'll all solve problems together, and outsiders will think you're a bunch of superheroes.

day 55 checklist

_____ do your morning ritual

_____ smile at yourself in the mirror

_____ do something active

_____ don't consume negative news

_____ listen to something positive, inspirational or instructional

_____ whenever someone irritates you, practice controlling your response

_____ do something you love

_____ do what you wrote down on DAY 40, to be a leader, and what you wrote on DAY 45, to become who you need to be to realize the company's vision

_____ read DAY 55 so you can be purposefully-positive at work

add this if it's a **work day:**

_____ smile at, and greet every person you pass today at work

_____ give yourself and your employees some DO NOT DISTURB time

_____ be in character

_____ make all emails you send to employees follow DAY 33

_____ help your employees to be more active at work

day 56

Turn off all the social media notifications on your phone and computer. You don't want to find out immediately that someone liked or commented on your post. You don't want to know in real time when someone follows you, or friend requests you.

Go into each app's settings and turn off all the notifications. Then decide on two or three specific times during the day that you'll take ten minutes to check.

This might be painful at first, but see how much more you get done today. See how fast you get moving on your priorities. See how much time you're able to give back to yourself and your own goals. **And don't go back to the way things were until you give this a chance during the rest of the time of this challenge.**

day 56 checklist

_____ do your morning ritual

_____ smile at yourself in the mirror

_____ do something active

_____ don't consume negative news

_____ listen to something positive, inspirational or instructional

_____ whenever someone irritates you, practice controlling your response

_____ do something you love

_____ do what you wrote down on DAY 40, to be a leader, and what you wrote on DAY 45, to become who you need to be to realize the company's vision

_____ turn off social media notifications on your phone & computer

add this if it's a **work day:**

_____ smile at, and greet every person you pass today at work

_____ give yourself and your employees some DO NOT DISTURB time

_____ be in character and include being purposefully-positive

_____ make all emails you send to employees follow DAY 33

_____ help your employees to be more active at work

notes & ideas

week 9

month 3 checklist

here's what you'll do regularly & consistently

_____ help your employees' jobs support their personal goals *(from DAY 8 & DAY 15)*

_____ help your employees support each other's personal goals *(from DAY 9)*

_____ keep DAY 10 in mind while you help your employees to achieve company goals

_____ make your position support your personal goals *(from DAY 16)*

_____ keep working and moving forward on ways to let your employees do their jobs independently (places for you to get updates, written procedures, authorization, resources, giving instructions & expectations clearly – *from DAY 18-20*)

_____ get to know your employees and find ways to show you care about them and the things that are important to them *(from DAY 22)*

_____ keep working on ways to help each of your employees show off their other talents at work, and put the plans in place so everyone gets a chance to shine by the end of the challenge *(reference lists made on DAY 29 & DAY 32)*

_____ look for ways to give recognition for assignments/projects *(from DAY 41)*

_____ use rewards effectively *(from DAY 42)*

_____ follow through on your employee wellness plan *(from DAY 44)*

_____ follow through on your employee development plan *(from DAY 46)*

_____ be consistent - and make sure management is too *(from DAY 50)*

_____ know what to do about low-performers *(from DAY 51)*

week 9 checklist

here's what you'll do at least 1 time each this week

_____ ask an employee, "how are you?", and then listen to the answer, give a thoughtful response, and follow up later (if applicable)

_____ sincerely thank an employee for his/her unique contribution to the company (you want everyone who works for you – or at least those you can come in contact with – to hear this from you by the end of the challenge)

_____ _____ _____ prepare to work on a personal goal the next morning

_____ _____ _____ work on a personal goal first thing in the morning

_____ do random acts of kindness for your employees

_____ visit your employees around work, and ask how they're doing and if there's anything they need

_____ write and mail a letter to an employee, thanking him/her for being part of the company, expressing specific things he/she has done well, his/her strengths, and things you admire about the employee's character (write enough of these each week so that all employees have received one from you by the end of the challenge)

day 57

You want a company full of people who are kind to each other. You want your company to be a place where people care for each other, look out for each other, and help each other to succeed.

You want each person there to walk into work every day and be greeted by friends. You want each person to say that your company is a place where he/she feels valued, supported, encouraged, and loved. You want your company to be a place where each person can come in to work with his/her own unique background, traits and ideas, and feel confident, safe and welcomed.

If you were only going to do one thing from this whole book, I hope this would be the page you tear out and put on your refrigerator. Because today you're going to start brainstorming a program to recognize and reward kindness. You're going to start watching out for all the nice, friendly, and helpful things your employees do for each other, and you're going to let them know you've noticed and that you appreciate it.

And while I think it will make a fantastic impact if you do the looking out and recognizing, I don't think you should stop there. I think everyone - in every position - should get involved in this. You want it to be something that spreads through every level, no matter how many people you've got there.

The company my cousin works for has each employee watch out for any good deed, helpfulness, or act of kindness from their coworkers, and then use an app to report it. Management gets notified through the app, and then the employee who was reported about gets points through the app that he/she can use to buy things from local vendors.

My one suggestion is that you reward both the person who did the kind act, *and* the person who reported it (and that may be happening in my cousin's company; I just didn't think to ask), but I love the idea, and you can take it right into your place, whether you use an app or not.

Think of a method that works for you and your company. You might have people reporting in a digital program, or you might have them sending emails/texts, or you might have them writing it down and tossing it in a bowl in your office.

And think of the reward. It could be recognition. It could be you making a big announcement during each meeting, where you share the kind things people have done for each other, and get everyone clapping. It could be points that accumulate and qualify the employee for a bonus, or a paid day off, or a Visa gift card, or whatever you can give. It could be something really meaningful, like a list that gets kept all year and put into a book for the employee, with all the things his/her coworkers reported. Or something like donations from the company to the employee's favorite charity.

And as far as kind deeds that qualify for recognition, I'd say – don't put a cap on it or a floor. I think absolutely anything that makes someone feel welcome, respected, valued, and cared for at work counts. Someone holding the elevator door, or helping pick up fallen papers, or going up and making an introduction, or sitting next to someone at lunch who was alone, or getting someone coffee, or taking time to explain a program, or being a listening ear on a bad day, or remembering to say, "happy birthday". Anything and everything, I think.

Get all of your employees actively looking for the good in each other. Get them reporting kindness about their managers; assistants; coworkers; employees. Encourage and celebrate it so much that you're giving out recognition like confetti.

I think this one thing alone will transform your whole company. This will affect everything – including your clients' experiences with your business. This will give you people that all the other fantastic people in the world want to work with. This one thing is what I'd pick as the most important, and I'm hoping everything you've done so far has set it up to be an even bigger success. So however you choose to do it is fine; just plan a way today so you can get going on it tomorrow.

---

*Here's just a little thing to consider, while you decide how to reward kindness. Although I really love the idea of giving recognition with things like bonuses, gift cards, or points to earn perks, I think you should do some research and thinking yourself about whether that would be the most effective way to continuously motivate and foster a true spirit of kindness for the sake of it. It's probably one of those things where it depends on the specifics, and how you set it up, so you might be able to create a really special thing with monetary-type rewards that go to the employee. I just wanted to toss this out there, so you can think about it and decide what's best for you and your employees.

---

day 57 checklist

_____ do your morning ritual

_____ smile at yourself in the mirror

_____ do something active

_____ don't consume negative news

_____ listen to something positive, inspirational or instructional

_____ whenever someone irritates you, practice controlling your response

_____ do something you love

_____ do what you wrote down on DAY 40, to be a leader, and what you wrote on DAY 45, to become who you need to be to realize the company's vision

_____ plan a program for recognizing and rewarding kindness from your employees

add this if it's a **work day:**

_____ smile at, and greet every person you pass today at work

_____ give yourself and your employees some DO NOT DISTURB time

_____ be in character and include being purposefully-positive

_____ make all emails you send to employees follow DAY 33

_____ help your employees to be more active at work

day 58

Yesterday you made a plan for recognizing and rewarding your employees' acts of kindness, and for helping them to find the good in each other. Put your plan in place today!

day 58 checklist

_____ do your morning ritual

_____ smile at yourself in the mirror

_____ do something active

_____ don't consume negative news

_____ listen to something positive, inspirational or instructional

_____ whenever someone irritates you, practice controlling your response

_____ do something you love

_____ do what you wrote down on DAY 40, to be a leader, and what you wrote on DAY 45, to become who you need to be to realize the company's vision

add this if it's a **work day:**

_____ smile at, and greet every person you pass today at work

_____ give yourself and your employees some DO NOT DISTURB time

_____ be in character and include being purposefully-positive

_____ make all emails you send to employees follow DAY 33

_____ help your employees to be more active at work

_____ put your program for recognizing and rewarding kindness in place

day 59

Your employees want to change the world. They want to save the planet, and give back to mankind, and make a difference for a worthy cause, and if you help them to do all that with this job, you and your company will be just as richly rewarded.

We all want to do work that serves a higher purpose. You want that too. This will give you even more happiness, and more fulfillment, while you give it to your employees. And you don't have to make it something complicated or costly. I wrote a blog post to employees, to give them ideas for giving back with their jobs. Read it today and come up with something you can do:

https://www.elmoregroupinc.com/blog/2018/2/20/how-to-make-a-difference-with-your-job

You don't have to rush the planning of this one; just pick a small way to start, do it as soon as possible, and then keep finding ways to regularly give back as a company.

day 59 checklist

_____ do your morning ritual

_____ smile at yourself in the mirror

_____ do something active

_____ don't consume negative news

_____ listen to something positive, inspirational or instructional

_____ whenever someone irritates you, practice controlling your response

_____ do something you love

_____ do what you wrote down on DAY 40, to be a leader, and what you wrote on DAY 45, to become who you need to be to realize the company's vision

_____ read the blog post and think of ways to give back as a company

add this if it's a **work day:**

_____ smile at, and greet every person you pass today at work

_____ give yourself and your employees some DO NOT DISTURB time

_____ be in character and include being purposefully-positive

_____ make all emails you send to employees follow DAY 33

_____ help your employees to be more active at work

day 60

Give back in your personal life. You can make and keep some kits in your car for the homeless, or donate regularly to your favorite charity, or participate in a fundraiser event now and then, or go sit and talk with someone in a nursing home sometimes, or send a card to someone who could use a lift, or pick up some groceries for your neighbor one day.

You just got a bunch of ideas yesterday, so think of something doable you can start with, write it down today, and then do it as soon as possible.

And please keep in mind: We can all only do what we can. There will never be a shortage of need in the world, and you could kill yourself trying to make a dent in it and never be able to. You're one person, and you've probably already got plenty of other things on your plate, so please don't turn this into something that fills you with guilt over how little you're doing to save the world, or something that stretches you so thin you end up snapping and spending a month in a padded room.

This is to help others, yes, but it's also something for *you*. It can be really simple, and it can be done every now and then, as you're able. It should be something that gives you energy, and gives you a good feeling about the world, and makes you feel gratitude, and contributes to your happiness, and gives you even more love for people.

So do this one with good judgement, like everything else.

day 60 checklist

_____ do your morning ritual

_____ smile at yourself in the mirror

_____ do something active

_____ don't consume negative news

_____ listen to something positive, inspirational or instructional

_____ whenever someone irritates you, practice controlling your response

_____ do something you love

_____ do what you wrote down on DAY 40, to be a leader, and what you wrote on DAY 45, to become who you need to be to realize the company's vision

_____ give back regularly in your personal life

add this if it's a **work day:**

_____ smile at, and greet every person you pass today at work

_____ give yourself and your employees some DO NOT DISTURB time

_____ be in character and include being purposefully-positive

_____ make all emails you send to employees follow DAY 33

_____ help your employees to be more active at work

day 61

Back on DAY 54, you asked your employees to anonymously submit their answers to this question: "What would make me a better [*your position/title*] for you?" It's been a week, and now it's time to start reading. Before you get into it though, just be reminded of the rules:

NO freaking out, getting discouraged, or getting mad about criticism. There can be NO negative consequences to this whole exercise. And NO getting conceited or deciding to coast if there's praise. Stay humble, stay objective, and use the answers to make changes in yourself and your behavior that will benefit everyone there, starting with you.

You're getting valuable information, so treat it that way. Make notes of all the changes you'll make, actions you'll take, and good things you already do that you can be more purposeful about from now on. Pay extra attention to any of the same answers. Think about whether different answers have similar, underlying themes.

And listen – yes – you might get some left-field responses. You might get crazy, entitled answers. Or answers from people who didn't take it seriously or weren't sure how to answer seriously without feeling awkward. Be humble, and objective, and use good judgement, so you'll know how to tell the difference. And realize that you can still learn things from those responses.

And remember – you already made yourself look fantastic for being brave enough and caring enough to ask for all this. Now go get reading, take lots of notes, and act accordingly!

day 61 checklist

_____ do your morning ritual

_____ smile at yourself in the mirror

_____ do something active

_____ don't consume negative news

_____ listen to something positive, inspirational or instructional

_____ whenever someone irritates you, practice controlling your response

_____ do something you love

_____ do what you wrote down on DAY 40, to be a leader, and what you wrote on DAY 45, to become who you need to be to realize the company's vision

add this if it's a **work day:**

_____ smile at, and greet every person you pass today at work

_____ give yourself and your employees some DO NOT DISTURB time

_____ be in character and include being purposefully-positive

_____ make all emails you send to employees follow DAY 33

_____ help your employees to be more active at work

_____ read all the responses to the question you asked on DAY 54, take notes, and use them to be better in your role

day 62

Today's topic is performance evaluations, and if that makes you want to yawn and check your watch, I understand. I know they can sometimes seem like a chore, or an interruption, or something you only need to think about when it's time to get them over with.

But you can make performance evaluations so much more. You can make them positively impact your employees' satisfaction, and engagement, and motivation, and performance, and today you'll learn how with this article:

https://prosky.co/talkingtalent/articles/how-to-conduct-performance-reviews-advice-from-employees

day 62 checklist

_____ do your morning ritual

_____ smile at yourself in the mirror

_____ do something active

_____ don't consume negative news

_____ listen to something positive, inspirational or instructional

_____ whenever someone irritates you, practice controlling your response

_____ do something you love

_____ do what you wrote down on DAY 40, to be a leader, and what you wrote on DAY 45, to become who you need to be to realize the company's vision

_____ read the article about how to do performance evaluations

add this if it's a **work day:**

_____ smile at, and greet every person you pass today at work

_____ give yourself and your employees some DO NOT DISTURB time

_____ be in character and include being purposefully-positive

_____ make all emails you send to employees follow DAY 33

_____ help your employees to be more active at work

_____ do whatever you identified to be better in your role for your employees

day 63

Back on DAY 5 we talked about how your employees could use their jobs at your company to reach their own personal goals, and why it's in your best interest for them to do that. Today we'll start something else to help your employees achieve goals with this job, and we'll do it by giving them connections. Here's how:

(1) Today, think about each of your employees and their personal goals, and make a quick list (there's space on the next page).

(2) Think about other people you know. People who have accomplished the things your employees want to accomplish. People who know other people your employees should know. People who know how to do things your employees want to learn.

(3) Write a name next to each employee's name.

(4) One-by-one, with each employee, prepare to make the connection. Reach out to the person you know, and let that person know you have an employee who wants to accomplish whatever-it-is, and that you thought this person could be a great mentor/advice-giver/connection, and ask if it would be okay to give their contact information to your employee (or if they have certain information public, like email address, social media sites, etc., just let them know you'll give their public info to your employee, and tell them your employee's name).

(5) When you have the go-ahead from your contact (or if you're just giving public contact info), pass the information along to your employee and tell him/her that you thought of this person as a great connection for them, since they want to accomplish whatever-the-goal-is, and that you've already reached out to this person to make it an easy in.

(6) Repeat with each employee on your list until you've connected each one with someone.

And no, you don't have to do this in one day! This is probably going to be something you pick away at, **so just come back to your list once a week and do what you can until it's all done.**

day 63 checklist

_____ do your morning ritual

_____ smile at yourself in the mirror

_____ do something active

_____ don't consume negative news

_____ listen to something positive, inspirational or instructional

_____ whenever someone irritates you, practice controlling your response

_____ do something you love

_____ do what you wrote down on DAY 40, to be a leader, and what you wrote on DAY 45, to become who you need to be to realize the company's vision

_____ work on giving each employee a valuable connection with someone

add this if it's a **work day:**

_____ smile at, and greet every person you pass today at work

_____ give yourself and your employees some DO NOT DISTURB time

_____ be in character and include being purposefully-positive

_____ make all emails you send to employees follow DAY 33

_____ help your employees to be more active at work

_____ do whatever you identified to be better in your role for your employees

notes & ideas

week 10

week 10 checklist

here's what you'll do at least 1 time each this week

_____ ask an employee, "how are you?", and then listen to the answer, give a thoughtful response, and follow up later (if applicable)

_____ sincerely thank an employee for his/her unique contribution to the company (you want everyone who works for you – or at least those you can come in contact with – to hear this from you by the end of the challenge)

_____ _____ _____ prepare to work on a personal goal the next morning

_____ _____ _____ work on a personal goal first thing in the morning

_____ do random acts of kindness for your employees

_____ visit your employees around work, and ask how they're doing and if there's anything they need

_____ write and mail a letter to an employee, thanking him/her for being part of the company, expressing specific things he/she has done well, his/her strengths, and things you admire about the employee's character (write enough of these each week so that all employees have received one from you by the end of the challenge)

_____ work at connecting each employee with a person you know who could give advice/be a mentor/etc. for that employee's personal goal (your list is on DAY 63)

day 64

One of my friends mentioned something to me a while back, and it's on my mind today, so let me pass it on to you:

She was talking about her job at the time; telling me about what she did, and how she liked it. And she said, "yeah, there's not a ton of stuff for me to do though, so I'm there forty hours a week, but if I get all my work done, I'll run out of things to do before the end of the week and my boss would think I don't do anything. So I have to try to space all my work out. The other people I work with have to do the same thing."

Does that seem a little backwards to you too? It stuck with me, and I've thought over it a lot since. If it makes you start to get nervous, I don't blame you, because I think it's more of a common scenario than we might realize. Since that one conversation, I've heard other people mention similar things about their jobs, and it reminded me of jobs I had where I didn't have enough work to fill every hour I was supposed to be there, and how I desperately tried to look busy every second, so my boss wouldn't get upset with me or decide I was expendable. And now I have an idea of how we can use this, and it's going to take a certain mindset from you:

In the past you might have had the opinion that you pay people for their time, but not anymore. **You pay people for RESULTS – not time.** You pay people to get things done, done (exceptionally-) well, and done as soon as they can possibly be done without sacrificing any quality. So here's what I think you start doing:

Celebrate the people who get more done (and done well) in less time. Start paying attention, and making a big, happy deal out of it, and let everyone else see it happen. And tell everyone how much you value that, so they won't be under the misconception that you're paying for bodies to fill a room for certain hours, and worry any longer that they'll be in trouble or considered useless if they finish all their work.

Then you can give options, so when people complete projects, they can start on other things that will benefit them, you, and the company.

> You could have a list of bonus projects for people to work on. Maybe certain ones could even come with an actual bonus!

> You could teach everyone the basics of selling for your company, and give every position the chance to get a commission on top of their regular pay, by making calls, making posts, or writing emails after they get the rest of their work done.

You could have resources available for personal development and training time, so people can use their extra time to study the skill or attribute they'd like to work on.

You could let them shadow each other with their extra time, to help everyone learn each other's roles and how to support each other more.

You could let them take turns shadowing *you*, to learn your role and how to support you in it more.

You could encourage them to take time just to sit and think. They could brainstorm ideas for the company's goals, their own role, or some challenge they're having in their personal life or at work, and write out their thoughts and ideas.

You could have them going around looking for people in the company who they can help, or give encouragement to, or do some act of kindness for.

You could have them volunteer in the community (on company time), or stay at work but work on a project to give back (like making Christmas cards for the local nursing home, or blankets for the hospital, or hygiene kits for the homeless shelter, etc.).

You could pick and choose from this, or do a combination of all of them, or something totally different, but the point is that extra time can be a wonderful thing for you, your company, and your employees, if you use it well.

I was on a jobsite once for a construction company, and the guy I was working with told me we would have to "take our time" with our assignment for the day, because it was a simple job, and going at a steady pace would keep him from getting the number of hours he needed for his paycheck.

I mean – what if you do celebrate results so much that you let people go home early in cases like that… and with a full day's pay? I think, you might have paid it anyway if not, but you might have been paying for the wrong things. I think if you consider paying for *results*; and I think if you even consider that you're paying for things like honesty, integrity, kindness, character – if you even set people up in a way, to give you those things - it'll pay you back with interest.

day 64 checklist

_____ do your morning ritual

_____ smile at yourself in the mirror

_____ do something active

_____ don't consume negative news

_____ listen to something positive, inspirational or instructional

_____ whenever someone irritates you, practice controlling your response

_____ do something you love

_____ do what you wrote down on DAY 40, to be a leader, and what you wrote on DAY 45, to become who you need to be to realize the company's vision

add this if it's a work day:

_____ smile at, and greet every person you pass today at work

_____ give yourself and your employees some DO NOT DISTURB time

_____ be in character and include being purposefully-positive

_____ make all emails you send to employees follow DAY 33

_____ help your employees to be more active at work

_____ do whatever you identified to be better in your role for your employees

_____ start celebrating quality work getting done - not time spent

day 65

Have you ever heard the saying, "people don't quit jobs; they quit bosses"? When I first heard it, I'd already quit a few jobs, and I realized the statement rang true for me.

The bosses I quit were good people. They had the best intentions. I just think that under the pressure to make sure we got it all done, they lost the ability to manage their fears. And I can feel for them. I wish sometimes that I could go back and be more understanding, and not take it so personally.

And since I can't at this point, I'd rather help you to help your own managers. If you're doing this challenge and there's no one between you and any other employee you're leading, then you only need to worry about you, and if you're committed to this challenge, you're doing great.

But if there's even one manager between you and your other employees, I would consider that relationship, and how to make it one that brings out the best in everyone. You want each of your managers to sincerely care for each person he/she is responsible for. You want them to know each of them, and understand their strengths, and understand their challenges, and understand what they care about, and understand what motivates them, and understand the type of environment they each need to thrive. You want them to see the good in each person, and believe in their abilities, and give them belief in themselves, and inspire them to be better, and give them opportunities to grow.

There's so much to navigate, and it can be so hard to do without getting afraid and pushing away the people they're supposed to be leading and caring for. So today, consider what doing this challenge has done for you, and whether it would be something your managers could benefit from as well. They're also in the position of being both a boss and an employee, and there's a second challenge to employees (called, *Use Your Job: A 90-Day Challenge*) that I think they would really get a lot from too.

Here's where you can get both books: https://www.amazon.com/author/joanelmore

You want to start a ripple-effect in your company, with each person bringing out the best in everyone else. You want a company full of people who are so fantastic and magnetic, that the best talent out there hunts you down and begs to be part of what you're building. And each employee's direct manager will have a huge influence over whether that happens.

day 65 checklist

_____ do your morning ritual

_____ smile at yourself in the mirror

_____ do something active

_____ don't consume negative news

_____ listen to something positive, inspirational or instructional

_____ whenever someone irritates you, practice controlling your response

_____ do something you love

_____ do what you wrote down on DAY 40, to be a leader, and what you wrote on DAY 45, to become who you need to be to realize the company's vision

_____ consider how to improve your employees' relationship with their managers

add this if it's a **work day:**

_____ smile at, and greet every person you pass today at work

_____ give yourself and your employees some DO NOT DISTURB time

_____ be in character and include being purposefully-positive

_____ make all emails you send to employees follow DAY 33

_____ help your employees to be more active at work

_____ do whatever you identified to be better in your role for your employees

day 66

Remember Show-and-Tell in school? You stood at the front of the classroom and held up your stuffed dinosaur, or your collection of painted rocks, or the trophy you got for basketball, or the pictures of your parents in their swimsuits during summer break, and you told everyone about yourself, and your experiences, and the things that mattered to you, and the things that made you unique.

Let's bring back Show-and-Tell, and give each of your employees the same feeling of being special, and interesting, and unique; and give all of them a chance to get to know each other a little more, and in a fun way. We'll just revise it a little to make it doable.

You're going to highlight each employee, one-at-a-time, once a month (you could do it as often as you want, but every thirty days or so seems manageable to me). During this challenge you'll do this for one person, **but once you start, you'll need to make sure to continue it, even after the challenge is over**.

Here's how you'll do it:

(1) Today, make a list of all your employees, and then pick a name to start with.

(2) Take the next week or so to gather the info. Find out the employee's hobbies, talents, interests. Ask your employee some questions about himself/herself (you could have an informal form you give out for this, with questions like, "what's got you really excited lately?", "what would you love to do for the world?", "what would you want people to know about you?", etc.) Ask his/her coworkers to tell you what they admire about the employee (maybe list those anonymously, but you can decide that).

(3) Once a month, post the information and a great picture for all to see. You could put it in the breakroom, or other employee-only areas, or display it where everyone who walks into the building can appreciate it.

(4) Repeat the process each month, and celebrate a new employee.

You could do so much with this. You could have an actual celebration each time, with cake and everything, and have people (you included) share things they appreciate and admire about the employee.

You could keep all the stuff you put up for each employee, and hang them all up together somewhere (just in a different place than the designated, special spot for that month's employee highlight), to keep everyone reminded about how interesting they all are, and give new employees a way to learn more about their coworkers.

You could have everyone write down the things they appreciate and admire about the employee, and then put them all into a folder, book, or box to give to him/her.

You could have a different special gift to give each month's employee (just make it the same thing for everyone, and make sure everyone gets a turn).

You could make this a one-time thing for each employee, or when you've done a highlight for every single person there, you could start all over again with each name, and find more things to post and celebrate about them.

All by itself, maybe this wouldn't be a game-changer. But you're layering it with all the other parts of this challenge, and making it just one more of many ways to care about and take an interest in the people who work for you, and bring all of you closer together.

However you choose to do this, I really think it'll be something special. I think our first-grade teachers were onto something. And some things just never get old.

---

*Ahem – I suddenly feel like I have to toss out a little side-note, even though this probably doesn't need to be said. Just make sure that – you know – you don't pick people to highlight based on who's performing the best, and don't hold out on anyone based on poor performance. This isn't a reward for working well, it's a show of appreciation for being part of the company.

I'd make the selection totally random. Stick all the names in a jar, pull one out blind, do the highlight for that person, and leave that name out of the jar so that next time someone else who hasn't gotten a turn will get picked. You might select someone who's been late seven times this month, or who always seems to go at half-speed, or who *just can't figure it out, dammit*, and you'll celebrate him/her with enthusiasm anyway.

day 66 checklist

_____ do your morning ritual

_____ smile at yourself in the mirror

_____ do something active

_____ don't consume negative news

_____ listen to something positive, inspirational or instructional

_____ whenever someone irritates you, practice controlling your response

_____ do something you love

_____ do what you wrote down on DAY 40, to be a leader, and what you wrote on DAY 45, to become who you need to be to realize the company's vision

_____ make a list of all your employees, and choose one at random to do the first highlight for

_____ take the next week to prep and get info about the employee to highlight

add this if it's a **work day:**

_____ smile at, and greet every person you pass today at work

_____ give yourself and your employees some DO NOT DISTURB time

_____ be in character and include being purposefully-positive

_____ make all emails you send to employees follow DAY 33

_____ help your employees to be more active at work

_____ do whatever you identified to be better in your role for your employees

day 67

I learned something recently about motivation. Ready for it? I bet it'll blow your mind:

We aren't all motivated by the same things.

I know, I know, it's earth-shattering news. But here's the part that really got me thinking:

All of us are basically motivated by *one of two* things, and those are (1) pleasure, or (2) prevention of pain. And that reminds me of when I was eighteen.

When I was eighteen, I found in dismay that the end of high school had made me a little soft. ...Physically, I mean. I had some pesky pounds that I wanted to get rid of, and I couldn't seem to stick to any diet or exercise plan, so I thought of a sure way to light a fire under my feet and start shedding: I'd terrorize myself away from the kitchen and out to my treadmill on the porch.

So I found pictures of extreme cases of obesity and hung them around my room. I taped them to the fridge and pantry, along with words I'd cut out of magazines. "FAT", "DON'T DO IT", "NO, NO, NO". I prominently displayed my largest-sized clothes at the front of my closet, and drew little sad faces to attach to them.

(I was eighteen, okay? My three-year-old ate a ball of playdoh the other day. Kids do weird things before they figure things out.)

Every time I went into my room or the kitchen, I was assaulted with warnings, and I fully expected to be scared straight. But would you believe it – my plan wasn't working. Not at all. In fact, I was going to the fridge *more*, it seemed. I was *gaining* weight. In total dismay and desperation, I gathered more pictures and words of warning, and found new places in the house to put them.

Now whenever I opened my closet, or got a glass of water at midnight, or took my towel off the rack, or opened a book, or lifted the toilet lid – I'd get a jolting reminder of an unwanted future.

At this point, I have a few theories about why my plan didn't work for me, but there's only one we need to get into today: I was trying to motivate myself with something that is not at all motivating to me. I was trying to pump myself up with thoughts of disaster, when disaster really doesn't elicit a rise.

And thinking about it now makes me think about your employees. Each of them is motivated by either pleasure or prevention of pain, and chances are – they don't all light up for the same one. And if you're only speaking to one side, you're probably leaving a bunch of people out and diminishing your own results.

This will be kind of a longer-term thing to continuously think about and figure out, but **you'll want to learn how each of your employees is motivated, and speak the right language when you talk to him/her, so you can keep your whole team stoked to perform at their peak.** So first, just start observing. When you talk to people, and when you hear them talking, pay attention to how they word things, and even to their tone.

Let's say Ned consistently expresses things like, "I think I'm going to trade my car in soon, before it gives me any more problems,"; and "Ugh, I hope this storm doesn't mess up my new trees,"; and "I better cut down on the sugar; I don't want to pack on any more weight this year." Chances are, he's motivated by avoiding pain; by keeping an undesirable outcome from happening.

And let's say Suzy sounds like this: "I'm going to trade in my car soon – it'll be so nice to have something reliable!"; and "I hope my new trees will get through this storm,"; and "I'm cutting down on the sugar; I want to get healthy this year!" She's most likely motivated by pleasure; the outcome she does want to happen.

I'm like Suzy, myself. If at eighteen, I'd taped pictures of fitness models all over the house, and attached one to the wall in front of my treadmill with a sign that said, "THIS CAN BE YOU!!" – I probably would've been so busy charging down my dream, that I wouldn't have remembered we had a refrigerator. …But I didn't know this about myself back then. And I can remember times in jobs where my boss didn't realize this about me either, and would try to scare me into action.

"If we don't get this contract, it's gonna be a real tough ride the rest of the year."

"We need to keep this project from losing any more money or there won't be any profits left for bonuses."

"If you can't make more calls during your shifts, you're not going to have job security here."

I hear the words, and I mean – it's serious; I get it. But it just doesn't light me up. Ned would leap at that kind of talk though, and that's why you can't just say it once, in one way.

For your pleasure-people, use language that pumps them up about what's possible; what the reward is; what bright, shining outcome is just ready and waiting if they do certain things and push through this part. Tell them how great it will be for them, you, and everyone there if you all win the contract, or wow this client, or come in with profits to spare.

For the people who are motivated by keeping pain away, get them all rallying for your cause by explaining the hurdles you're trying to get through, and the potential consequences you're trying to avoid, and ask for their help in protecting everyone there from those.

When you've got everyone together in a meeting, and you're trying to motivate them all to embrace a procedure change, or get behind a new system, or launch forward on your focus for the quarter, speak to both sides and cover all your bases. Tell them how wonderful this will be for everyone, and paint a picture of all the great things that will come out of it. And explain the challenges, and the negative things you're trying to avoid, and ask for their help in preventing those.

This whole subject has me thinking about my kids and how often I try to get them moving on my objective by speaking to both of them the same way.

"If you don't get in the car now, we won't go to the park."

"If you brush your teeth now, I'll let you stay up a little later."

"If you color the floor again, no crayons ever."

I usually choose one side of it, and stick to that. Sometimes it just feels like there's no time or fuel in me to think of everything constantly. But when I do that, one person starts cooperating, and the other keeps running for a puddle, or rolling on the bathmat, or sketching on the tile, and each kid's response varies with the method I choose.

You want *everyone* motivated, at the same time. I think if you take the extra time for this, you'll avoid a scenario where half the room is detached during your locker room speech. I think speaking to each person's style this way will help everyone there to feel connected to, inspired by, and motivated about your call to action. I think you'll love the results.

day 67 checklist

_____ do your morning ritual

_____ smile at yourself in the mirror

_____ do something active

_____ don't consume negative news

_____ listen to something positive, inspirational or instructional

_____ whenever someone irritates you, practice controlling your response

_____ do something you love

_____ do what you wrote down on DAY 40, to be a leader, and what you wrote on DAY 45, to become who you need to be to realize the company's vision

_____ keep prepping for your first employee highlight (it's in six days)

add this if it's a **work day:**

_____ smile at, and greet every person you pass today at work

_____ give yourself and your employees some DO NOT DISTURB time

_____ be in character and include being purposefully-positive

_____ make all emails you send to employees follow DAY 33

_____ help your employees to be more active at work

_____ do whatever you identified to be better in your role for your employees

_____ learn how each of your employees is motivated and tailor your language

day 68

You might only have to switch up your style of speech a couple ways to motivate each of your employees, but today we're going to talk about something they each personally identify with; something that hits each of them at their core, and drives their decisions. …And that something comes in way more variations than the number of people in your building.

The subject for the next two days is *values*. Mastering motivation will drastically increase your results, yes. You'll have people energetically working to achieve your desired outcomes. But if you can also figure out how to help those people to personally connect with your company's mission and vision – at a gut-level, *this feels right* kind of place – I think you'll leave your competition in the dust and quickly become something legendary.

So let's get into it! What are values, exactly? I went to the dictionary (because I want to get this totally right), and it told me that a person's values are his/her principles; the things he/she believes to be important in life.

Our principles are personal to us, and most often vary with each person. Even when we share certain values with others, the degree of importance we give them, and the reasons behind their importance to us often varies. We're all different. Our personalities, and life experiences are different. There's not a set number of values per person. And that can make the rest of this a little bit of a challenge.

Because you want to do your best to learn each of your employee's values. Even just *one* value, for each person. Someone there might have values of *family, creativity,* and *kindness.* For someone else it might be *adventure, change,* and *freedom.* Or *security, stability, friendship, respect, achievement, challenge,* and on and on.

You could find this out by asking. Maybe with, "what things are most important to you in life?" or "What things do you believe in?" (and maybe you could do this at the same time you gather information for each employee highlight!). Or you can be observant, and learn them over time by seeing how people act and what they choose to do with their time, hearing what they talk about, and watching for what gets them excited.

The guy who constantly uses his days off to kayak every river in the country might value *nature, fun, freedom,* or *autonomy.* The girl who spends all her nights and weekends training as a boxer might value *challenge, achievement, respect,* or *independence.*

You want to know what your employees feel connected to. Today, think about how you can learn, and tomorrow we'll talk about what to do with this.

day 68 checklist

_____ do your morning ritual

_____ smile at yourself in the mirror

_____ do something active

_____ don't consume negative news

_____ listen to something positive, inspirational or instructional

_____ whenever someone irritates you, practice controlling your response

_____ do something you love

_____ do what you wrote down on DAY 40, to be a leader, and what you wrote on DAY 45, to become who you need to be to realize the company's vision

_____ keep prepping for your first employee highlight (it's in five days)

add this if it's a work day:

_____ smile at, and greet every person you pass today at work

_____ give yourself and your employees some DO NOT DISTURB time

_____ be in character and include being purposefully-positive

_____ make all emails you send to employees follow DAY 33

_____ help your employees to be more active at work

_____ do whatever you identified to be better in your role for your employees

_____ think about how you might start learning each of your employee's values

day 69

When I was twenty-five, I started looking for a house to buy. I had a small budget, and not a lot of room for options, but I was excited to get a little place of my own. My realtor was a kind lady who was endlessly-patient with my inexperience, and she set out to help me find the perfect house.

She spent evenings and weekends, showing me property-after-property. Each one was in my budget; each one had way more going for it than I'd expected to be able to afford. She made sure each place was in a safe location, and didn't have high association fees, and wouldn't require any renovations. She spent a while; over six months. Because I couldn't put my finger on it, but each place felt like someone else's house. No place was *the* place.

Until finally, one was. It was one we stumbled on by a fortunate chain of events; one I begged to look at. A tiny, bank-repossessed half of a duplex on a quiet circle. We walked in and took in the cramped, outdated kitchen; the awkward, mismatched tile all over the floor; the disgusting carpets in the two bedrooms, and the strange sculptures all over the walls.

My realtor's eyebrow had been arched since we walked in, and she was nodding with her mouth in a tight line. "Okay," she finally said, "This one would need some work, probably."

I was beaming and dancing in excitement. "I love it; I want it! This is the one I want!"

She seemed shocked. It didn't make sense to want this mess of a place, when we'd looked at so many other ones that were in such better shape.

But so many times we don't make decisions based on what makes sense. This house just *felt* right. It was the place for me. And as I skipped through the rooms I could see my life here. I pictured starting out a marriage in this house; future kids playing in this yard. It felt right, and so it's where my husband and I live with our little daughters, eight years later while I write this book.

And here's the lesson from that: most of us let feelings be our guide when we make our biggest life choices. And our values influence the whole process.

When someone is suffering from a nagging feeling that their job isn't right for them; when they can't seem to be satisfied with any raises, or bonuses, or new titles – so often it's because whatever is being given doesn't line up (or seem to, anyway) with that employee's values. The employee may not even realize it; may not even be able to put a finger on what exactly is wrong. But it just doesn't feel right.

And on the flipside, when someone else is in a job that does align with his/her values, almost no amount of worry from their parents, or skepticism from their friends, or coupon-clipping, or humble living can dampen their drive to go there and be part of it. It just feels right.

You want each person in your company to feel that connection and harmony between their work and position here, and the principles they value for their life.

You're already doing a lot with this challenge that will help your employees' jobs to give them things like *independence*, and *kindness*, and *service*, and *progression*, and *friendship*, which are all pretty commonly-held values for many people. And as you learn each person's values in more detail, you can find ways to help their jobs to align with those also, and even more.

It might be through additional/new assignments.

Or training, seminars, or classes.

Or an offer to relocate to a branch in a different area.

Or a schedule change.

Or opportunities for travel, *or* for staying put more often.

Or a way to work more independently, or to do remote work.

Or a connection with someone in the company who lives in alignment with a certain value, and who can be a mentor.

It could also be by explaining your company's values in a way that helps your employees to connect with them, and feel how the company's values support and align with their own.

This is something I *highly* recommend prioritizing, and *highly* recommend that you give extra study-time to, so you can get more ideas and learn about it in-depth. This is where I'm leaving you, but there are experts out there who have this subject all figured out, and you want to hear whatever they're sharing. This could transform your whole place, and everyone in it.

day 69 checklist

_____ do your morning ritual

_____ smile at yourself in the mirror

_____ do something active

_____ don't consume negative news

_____ listen to something positive, inspirational or instructional

_____ whenever someone irritates you, practice controlling your response

_____ do something you love

_____ do what you wrote down on DAY 40, to be a leader, and what you wrote on DAY 45, to become who you need to be to realize the company's vision

_____ keep prepping for your first employee highlight (it's in four days)

add this if it's a **work day:**

_____ smile at, and greet every person you pass today at work

_____ give yourself and your employees some DO NOT DISTURB time

_____ be in character and include being purposefully-positive

_____ make all emails you send to employees follow DAY 33

_____ help your employees to be more active at work

_____ do whatever you identified to be better in your role for your employees

_____ think about how you might help your employees' jobs to align with their values

day 70

In one of my jobs, my boss asked each of us to write down what the company's mission statement meant to us personally, and then he collected all the answers and put them into a binder in the reception area, for waiting clients to read.

I've always thought that was such a great idea. I didn't even know what the mission statement was before that exercise, and instead of letting my first official meeting with it be at a glance, I had to really think about what it meant, and make it mean something to me.

And what a great way to let clients connect with the mission too, and get to know everyone in the company a little more. So many times after that, when I'd walk out to greet clients, they'd close the binder and smile as they told me they'd just been reading what I wrote.

Let's use that strategy today, and you'll tailor it to fit your employees and company.

(1) Ask each person to write down what your company's mission means to him/her, and send you the answer (make sure you give a deadline, and don't make it longer than a few days from now).

(2) Once you get all the answers, find a way to display them. It could be by putting them in a binder, or onto t-shirts, or making a framed collage for the wall, or making coffee mugs, or customizing the mousepads, or sewing them onto a flag to fly outside.

Whatever you choose to do, get personal with the mission statement. It might double as a way to make a great impression on your clients too, but that'll just be a bonus.

day 70 checklist

_____ do your morning ritual

_____ smile at yourself in the mirror

_____ do something active

_____ don't consume negative news

_____ listen to something positive, inspirational or instructional

_____ whenever someone irritates you, practice controlling your response

_____ do something you love

_____ do what you wrote down on DAY 40, to be a leader, and what you wrote on DAY 45, to become who you need to be to realize the company's vision

_____ keep prepping for your first employee highlight (it's in three days)

add this if it's a **work day:**

_____ smile at, and greet every person you pass today at work

_____ give yourself and your employees some DO NOT DISTURB time

_____ be in character and include being purposefully-positive

_____ make all emails you send to employees follow DAY 33

_____ help your employees to be more active at work

_____ do whatever you identified to be better in your role for your employees

_____ ask each of your employees to write down what the company's mission statement means to him/her, and send you the answer

notes & ideas

week 11

week 11 checklist

here's what you'll do at least 1 time each this week

_____ ask an employee, "how are you?", and then listen to the answer, give a thoughtful response, and follow up later (if applicable)

_____ sincerely thank an employee for his/her unique contribution to the company (you want everyone who works for you – or at least those you can come in contact with – to hear this from you by the end of the challenge)

_____ _____ _____ prepare to work on a personal goal the next morning

_____ _____ _____ work on a personal goal first thing in the morning

_____ do random acts of kindness for your employees

_____ visit your employees around work, and ask how they're doing and if there's anything they need

_____ write and mail a letter to an employee, thanking him/her for being part of the company, expressing specific things he/she has done well, his/her strengths, and things you admire about the employee's character (write enough of these each week so that all employees have received one from you by the end of the challenge)

_____ work at connecting each employee with a person you know who could give advice/be a mentor/etc. for that employee's personal goal (your list is on DAY 63)

day 71

I have a friend with a funny habit. She regularly asks people for their opinions, advice, or experiences, and the conversation will go something like this:

> *Friend:* "Hey when your son was this age [*gesturing to hers*], how did you get him to sleep at night?"
>
> "Well what I used to –"
>
> *Friend, interrupting*: "Because I've tried a ton of stuff; cereal in his bottle, a bath right before bedtime, I play quiet music, I *always* keep the same bedtime routine. I mean – what else can there be?!"
>
> "Yeah, that stuff is great! So what I did though was –"
>
> *Friend:* "You didn't put him in your bed, did you? I keep reading about how once you start that, they'll never want to sleep anywhere else. I don't know about you, but I need my own space at night!"

And it goes on like that. Sometimes my friend never even gets the answer she was looking for because by the time she's done talking, the time is up, or she's forgotten that the advice hasn't gotten to her yet, or the other person finally gets fed up and just starts agreeing with her. Listening to it makes me feel crazy. It's all I can do to keep from putting my finger to my lips and whispering in a mom-tone to *hush*.

And how does this apply to you, and your employees? Well – at times I've known bosses who remind me of my friend.

When they were asking for a status:

> *Boss:* "Hey what are you doing about the Fourth Street property?"
>
> "Oh yeah, I'm on that; I've got –"
>
> *Boss:* "Because we *can't* afford to drop the ball on that one, and I've got tight deadlines with the report. What you really should be doing is moving that up ahead of Elm Street, because that one's got some leeway with the timeline."

"Yeah, I was thinking the same thing, so –"

Boss: "Let's not delay that one. Just as soon as you can get that on my desk."

When they were training:

Boss: "Okay, you got any questions about that?"

"Well, I just –"

Boss: "Because this part of it can be a little tricky the first couple times; you'll need to get used to how this thing handles."

"Yeah, I'm good with that; I used one like it in my last job. I just –"

Boss: "Well don't assume you know everything about it; this is the newest model. We want to make sure everything here is the latest-greatest, you know, so your skills will have to be sharp. Lemmie show you over to the next part."

When they were looking for input in a meeting:

Boss: "Okay guys, so here's what we've got. What are your ideas on our best direction?"

[*A long-enough pause to draw a breath.*]

Boss: "Because I'm thinking we should probably go at it like this [*blah, blah, blah*], and I'd like to get your thoughts. …Anybody?"

"Sounds great."

I heard some wonderful advice recently, and today I'll pass it on to you:

Listen to everyone's input before you give your own.

Isn't that good? I know it might not seem groundbreaking, and I'm actually pretty sure you've already heard it, but today you're going to take it to heart like never before.

From now on, when you're going to ask for verbal input from any of your employees, you'll ask your question (or whatever it is), and then you'll bite your tongue, or dig your nails into your palms, or put a sticker over your lips, and you'll let each person you're in front of give their own answer.

And you'll listen to each one fully, and carefully, and without thinking about your reply, or how much you can't wait to give it. And you won't say a word about your own opinion, or idea, or that thing you *already know needs to be done, dammit.* You'll just listen.

Then you'll make each person feel good about his/her answer, by thanking them sincerely, and talking about the things you like about what they said.

If you're in a group, you'll give everyone else the chance to also give feedback to the person who just spoke.

And finally, when you've done all that, you can give your thoughts, or opinion, or advice, or instructions; and you might decide to say something different now that you've gotten to hear other perspectives, and you might keep it exactly the same as when you first asked the question.

But either way, this will go so far to show respect to your employees, and teach them how to show respect to each other, and build their respect for you.

day 71 checklist

_____ do your morning ritual

_____ smile at yourself in the mirror

_____ do something active

_____ don't consume negative news

_____ listen to something positive, inspirational or instructional

_____ whenever someone irritates you, practice controlling your response

_____ do something you love

_____ do what you wrote down on DAY 40, to be a leader, and what you wrote on DAY 45, to become who you need to be to realize the company's vision

_____ keep prepping for your first employee highlight (it's in two days)

add this if it's a work day:

_____ smile at, and greet every person you pass today at work

_____ give yourself and your employees some DO NOT DISTURB time

_____ be in character and include being purposefully-positive

_____ make all emails you send to employees follow DAY 33

_____ help your employees to be more active at work

_____ do whatever you identified to be better in your role for your employees

_____ listen to everyone's input, before you give your own

day 72

Do a search online of "people being kind", and watch at least two videos. And then for the rest of the day, purposely look around for all the examples you can find of goodness in the world, and in the people around you.

Small, simple acts of kindness totally count, so when you see someone smile, or give up their place in line, or stop to get a turtle out of the street, or discreetly get the toilet paper off of someone's shoe – it'll remind you how much good there really is everywhere.

Look for everything you can find today, write them down here, and read it tonight before you go to bed.

_____

_____

_____

_____

_____

_____

_____

day 72 checklist

_____ do your morning ritual

_____ smile at yourself in the mirror

_____ do something active

_____ don't consume negative news

_____ listen to something positive, inspirational or instructional

_____ whenever someone irritates you, practice controlling your response

_____ do something you love

_____ do what you wrote down on DAY 40, to be a leader, and what you wrote on DAY 45, to become who you need to be to realize the company's vision

_____ keep prepping for your first employee highlight (it's the day after tomorrow)

_____ do a search for "people being kind" and watch at least 2 videos

_____ look around today for every example of kindness/goodness you can find, and write it down, and then read it before you go to bed tonight

add this if it's a **work day:**

_____ smile at, and greet every person you pass today at work

_____ give yourself and your employees some DO NOT DISTURB time

_____ be in character and include being purposefully-positive

_____ make all emails you send to employees follow DAY 33

_____ help your employees to be more active at work

_____ do whatever you identified to be better in your role for your employees

_____ listen to everyone's input, before you give your own

day 73

You've got two things today:

(1) Finish prepping for your first employee highlight (from DAY 66) so you can do it tomorrow.

(2) Decide what you'll do with the answers everyone gave you, about what the company mission statement means to them, and move forward on it.

day 73 checklist

_____ do your morning ritual

_____ smile at yourself in the mirror

_____ do something active

_____ don't consume negative news

_____ listen to something positive, inspirational or instructional

_____ whenever someone irritates you, practice controlling your response

_____ do something you love

_____ do what you wrote down on DAY 40, to be a leader, and what you wrote on DAY 45, to become who you need to be to realize the company's vision

_____ finish prepping for your first employee highlight (it's tomorrow!)

_____ decide what you'll do with everyone's answers to what the company mission statement means to them (from DAY 70)

add this if it's a **work day:**

_____ smile at, and greet every person you pass today at work

_____ give yourself and your employees some DO NOT DISTURB time

_____ be in character and include being purposefully-positive

_____ make all emails you send to employees follow DAY 33

_____ help your employees to be more active at work

_____ do whatever you identified to be better in your role for your employees

_____ listen to everyone's input, before you give your own

day 74

Do your first employee highlight today!

day 74 checklist

_____ do your morning ritual

_____ smile at yourself in the mirror

_____ do something active

_____ don't consume negative news

_____ listen to something positive, inspirational or instructional

_____ whenever someone irritates you, practice controlling your response

_____ do something you love

_____ do what you wrote down on DAY 40, to be a leader, and what you wrote on DAY 45, to become who you need to be to realize the company's vision

add this if it's a **work day:**

_____ smile at, and greet every person you pass today at work

_____ give yourself and your employees some DO NOT DISTURB time

_____ be in character and include being purposefully-positive

_____ make all emails you send to employees follow DAY 33

_____ help your employees to be more active at work

_____ do whatever you identified to be better in your role for your employees

_____ listen to everyone's input, before you give your own

_____ do your first employee highlight

day 75

Remember back on DAY 10 when we talked about my friend in the sales position, who's managers constantly pulled rewards back out of reach if he got too close to achieving (or exceeding) the goals in a short amount of time?

Well there's more to the story, and I want to use it today. The companies he worked for all had some method for tracking how many people he talked to vs. how many sales he made. At some places it was a counter for all the times the front door opened (which was assumed to be a new potential customer in the building). At some it was a log, or a digital report. At others it was a manager watching and keeping score.

And don't get me wrong – those things should be measured. It's how you figure out when your customers are coming in, what makes them stay longer, what hours you should be open, how many employees you need to have at various times, what things are working and what aren't, etc., etc., etc. They're great tools.

The problem at my friend's companies was that these tracking methods were used as a way to punish sales people for "bad" ratios. If ten people walked in the store and only three of them bought something, my friend and his coworkers heard about it from management. If my friend approached twenty people himself, and only five of them bought something, he was really in trouble. And it's just got me thinking – maybe the companies he worked for would've had better odds if they didn't discourage their sales reps from approaching people.

And their particular methods were probably the exception, but when I think back to jobs I had where I was supposed to sell, I remember how much emphasis was put on closing the sale, and how much pressure I felt. If I talked to someone and they didn't buy, I felt terrible, and afraid of what my bosses would have to say. It made me want to avoid any situation where I could be told "no". If there were no prospects, I was off the hook (in my mind, anyway), so I talked to as few people as possible.

But years later, I had a job where there was no expectation placed on me for the number of sales made vs. the number of people I approached. If I had a great ratio, I'd be rewarded. But if not, no one would say anything, or discipline me. So I made it a game with myself, to see how many people I could offer extra services to. I got a lot of "no thank you"-s, but I didn't have negative consequences to worry about, so I kept asking more people. And I got a lot of "yes"-s. Those would never have happened if I hadn't asked, and I wouldn't have asked if I hadn't felt completely confident in my employer's support of my efforts. And with that on my mind, here's what we'll try today:

Let's help everyone to get over their fear of rejection.

Let's just have a trial run at this, and for a designated amount of time, instead of only celebrating closed sales, celebrate *action*. Celebrate *attempts*. Get everyone all pumped up by challenging them to take action with every single person they can, without negative consequences if a sale doesn't result. Maybe that means they'll go talk to anyone who wanders within sight of your place, or call on every possible prospect, or take the time to find out exactly what each potential customer is looking for, or go above and beyond to make a client's experience exceptional. Maybe that means someone will come up with a genius plan to get you all in front of way more prospects over time. Make it a contest, and track everyone's efforts.

Make a big deal about it. Get all excited, and announce each action while you write it on a board next to the person's name. When action results in a sale, pay the usual bonus, and cheer like crazy.

Just make the whole thing fun, and positive, and safe. I can vividly remember feeling crushed at times in my sales positions, and I remember the looks on my coworkers' faces when they were feeling it. It was utter defeat some days, and I just want to see what will happen if we fight defeat for a little bit.

Just try it for two weeks. Give yourself a couple days to plan it, and then set it up as an experiment, and tell your employees you want to play a game for a couple weeks to shake things up. If you don't like it after two weeks, go right back to the way things were.

But of course, after all that, I feel like I need to toss this in. Everything – everything – can be misunderstood, or taken too far, or be painted black and white when there's supposed to be grey all over. This does not mean you don't track, reward, or care about sales. This does not mean you don't analyze sales methods to find out what works and what doesn't, and help people to tweak their approach when it's needed. This does not mean that training, or good judgement, or tact, or integrity aren't needed.

You don't want your sales team chasing people down in the street, yelling at them to buy from you, putting it on their score card, and racing on to the next person. And you don't want them to stop trying to overcome objections, or stop trying to find a better solution for someone, or stop trying to build a relationship. And you don't want them to feel like skill doesn't matter, or that there's no need to make an effort with each person they get in front of.

This is going to take careful thought and planning, and good judgement. It'll take knowing your employees, and how to communicate it all to them, and how to set it up for them. But I think if you cover all of that, this could turn out to be a great thing for everyone, and especially you.

day 75 checklist

_____ do your morning ritual

_____ smile at yourself in the mirror

_____ do something active

_____ don't consume negative news

_____ listen to something positive, inspirational or instructional

_____ whenever someone irritates you, practice controlling your response

_____ do something you love

_____ do what you wrote down on DAY 40, to be a leader, and what you wrote on DAY 45, to become who you need to be to realize the company's vision

add this if it's a **work day:**

_____ smile at, and greet every person you pass today at work

_____ give yourself and your employees some DO NOT DISTURB time

_____ be in character and include being purposefully-positive

_____ make all emails you send to employees follow DAY 33

_____ help your employees to be more active at work

_____ do whatever you identified to be better in your role for your employees

_____ listen to everyone's input, before you give your own

_____ think about how you might help everyone to get over their fear of rejection around sales, and plan a two-week challenge

day 76

Shake things up with something totally fun and not-work-related. I'm springing it on you, so you might not be able to do it today, but plan today what you'll do and when (and try to make it happen within the next week).

You could have an ice cream truck park outside, so you can buy everyone sundaes, or have massage therapists come in and get the knots out of everyone's shoulders, or have a yoga instructor come in and help them all unwind, or play a game of dodgeball, or ask someone to come in and teach everyone to dance, or take a field trip to an art class, or get movie tickets and leave work early for a matinee.

Plan what you CAN do, plan when you'll do it, and set up a reminder so you won't forget.

day 76 checklist

_____ do your morning ritual

_____ smile at yourself in the mirror

_____ do something active

_____ don't consume negative news

_____ listen to something positive, inspirational or instructional

_____ whenever someone irritates you, practice controlling your response

_____ do something you love

_____ do what you wrote down on DAY 40, to be a leader, and what you wrote on DAY 45, to become who you need to be to realize the company's vision

_____ plan something fun and unexpected to do for your employees, write down the plan, and set up a reminder for when you want to set it up

add this if it's a **work day:**

_____ smile at, and greet every person you pass today at work

_____ give yourself and your employees some DO NOT DISTURB time

_____ be in character and include being purposefully-positive

_____ make all emails you send to employees follow DAY 33

_____ help your employees to be more active at work

_____ do whatever you identified to be better in your role for your employees

_____ listen to everyone's input, before you give your own

_____ think about how you might help everyone to get over their fear of rejection around sales, and plan a two-week challenge

day 77

You started thinking a couple days ago (on DAY 75) about how you might help everyone to get over their fear of rejection around sales. Today, put your plan in place, and try it out at least until the end of this challenge (you've only got two more weeks!).

day 77 checklist

_____ do your morning ritual

_____ smile at yourself in the mirror

_____ do something active

_____ don't consume negative news

_____ listen to something positive, inspirational or instructional

_____ whenever someone irritates you, practice controlling your response

_____ do something you love

_____ do what you wrote down on DAY 40, to be a leader, and what you wrote on DAY 45, to become who you need to be to realize the company's vision

add this if it's a work day:

_____ smile at, and greet every person you pass today at work

_____ give yourself and your employees some DO NOT DISTURB time

_____ be in character and include being purposefully-positive

_____ make all emails you send to employees follow DAY 33

_____ help your employees to be more active at work

_____ do whatever you identified to be better in your role for your employees

_____ listen to everyone's input, before you give your own

_____ put your plan in place to help everyone to get over their fear of rejection around sales, and do it for at least the next two weeks

notes & ideas

week 12

week 12 checklist

here's what you'll do at least 1 time each this week

_____ ask an employee, "how are you?", and then listen to the answer, give a thoughtful response, and follow up later (if applicable)

_____ sincerely thank an employee for his/her unique contribution to the company (you want everyone who works for you – or at least those you can come in contact with – to hear this from you by the end of the challenge)

_____ _____ _____ prepare to work on a personal goal the next morning

_____ _____ _____ work on a personal goal first thing in the morning

_____ do random acts of kindness for your employees

_____ visit your employees around work, and ask how they're doing and if there's anything they need

_____ write and mail a letter to an employee, thanking him/her for being part of the company, expressing specific things he/she has done well, his/her strengths, and things you admire about the employee's character (write enough of these each week so that all employees have received one from you by the end of the challenge)

_____ work at connecting each employee with a person you know who could give advice/be a mentor/etc. for that employee's personal goal (your list is on DAY 63)

day 78

In all of my past jobs, I had a pretty good understanding about what I was responsible for. My bosses made sure I started training for it on my first day. I was taught the company policies, and the procedures for my position, and I was told what was expected from me.

I just hardly ever had a complete grasp of what my coworkers did. All day, for five days each week, I'd sit right next to them, or bring files to their offices, or send them emails, or request things from them – and I only had a vague sense of what they were responsible for, and how their job description fit in with mine.

And I really think that kept me from using my position to its fullest potential. I really think I could have given so much more value and support to everyone, if I had just understood their jobs. So let's think about how you might help your employees to learn each other's responsibilities, and maximize the potential of each position there.

But first we need to get really clear about what this means. It's not that you have to teach everyone how to do every other job there. It's not that they all have to have the same skills. And it's not getting people to meddle in each other's jobs. It's not having people jumping in and taking over tasks for each other.

What this would look like is that each person there would do his/her own job, with a thorough understanding of where it fits in with everyone else's. Everyone would know how their actions and decisions affected everyone else there. They'd each be able to find ways to improve their specific operations. They'd all work better together, and work better for each other. And better for your company, and better for your clients, and better for you.

Can't you just see it? I'm getting stars in my eyes. So here's how you'll do it:

(1) **Decide what group(s) of people to include in this.** If yours is a small company, where everyone works closely together and you're over all of it, then it'll be easier to cover everything with everyone. If you've got a huge group of people, in multiple locations, or even in the same building, and/or you manage a certain department, you might have to make this doable by starting with a specific location, or department, or team.

(2) **Make a list of each position, and that position's responsibilities.**

(3) **Make a map for yourself, of the life of a project, and where it goes throughout the building during each phase.** You'll want to paint a clear picture of what each person does before handing it off to the next person, and all the different things happening at

once. So for example:

> Joey is a sales rep and he closes a sale and gets a signed contract and a check.
>
> Joey sends a copy of the contract and the check to Mary, in accounting, and the original contract to Janet, an administrator.
>
> Janet enters the new client information into the company's records, makes a file for the contract, and sends the customer a welcome packet.
>
> At the same time, Mary records and deposits the payment, and sets up for future billing, according to the contract.
>
> Janet sends the customer and job information to Mark, the project lead.
>
> Mark gets the work scheduled, and oversees the team while they complete it.
>
> Mark keeps Mary informed as certain steps get finished, so Mary can invoice the client accordingly.
>
> When the project is complete, Mark gets a sign-off from the customer and sends it to Mary, who sends a final invoice.
>
> When the invoice is paid, Mary informs Janet, who sends a Thank You packet and warranty information to the customer.

Etc. That's a rough summary, but can you see from that how many times the ball could be dropped if people forgot to communicate with each other? So yeah – get this sketched out with the particulars for your company, and highlight all the places where employees should be making sure to give clear and complete information and resources to each other.

(4) **Decide how you'll present this.** It could be at one meeting. It could be at a series of meetings. It could be through an (extensive) email, or series of them (but you'd want to make sure they get read). Or you could make a training packet, or training video.

(5) **Plan for how you could get your employees involved.** You might have them each think about and be ready to give suggestions for how their coworkers could support them in their roles (and you might decide to have them submit those to you first, so you can review and then present them at the meeting, or you might give time for a discussion, or

a combination of both). You might give each position/department a little side project of making a video or training packet for their coworkers, giving an overview of their responsibilities, their parts of a project, and a sneak peek into "a day in the life." You could let them take turns shadowing each other.

You could actually make this a really fun thing for everyone, if you want to get creative. And I think it'll be such a great thing for all of you.

day 78 checklist

_____ do your morning ritual

_____ smile at yourself in the mirror

_____ do something active

_____ don't consume negative news

_____ listen to something positive, inspirational or instructional

_____ whenever someone irritates you, practice controlling your response

_____ do something you love

_____ do what you wrote down on DAY 40, to be a leader, and what you wrote on DAY 45, to become who you need to be to realize the company's vision

_____ think about how to help everyone to learn each other's job descriptions

add this if it's a **work day:**

_____ smile at, and greet every person you pass today at work

_____ give yourself and your employees some DO NOT DISTURB time

_____ be in character and include being purposefully-positive

_____ make all emails you send to employees follow DAY 33

_____ help your employees to be more active at work

_____ do whatever you identified to be better in your role for your employees

_____ listen to everyone's input, before you give your own

_____ help everyone to get over their fear of rejection around sales

day 79

Take everything we talked about yesterday, and now think about how you can help your employees to learn your responsibilities. It could be with a meeting, or series of them. Or an email, or series of them. Or training materials you make. Or it could be by letting people take turns shadowing you.

However you decide to do this, I really think it'll reward you. Can you imagine how much better everyone will be at supporting your priorities, when they really understand what those are? Can you picture how fantastic it would be if someone came to you with an idea that was completely in line with your needs and objectives? Wouldn't it just be a dream come true if the quality and timing of everyone's work made your own feel almost effortless?

You can set everyone up to give these things to you, and all it takes is helping them to understand what you're responsible for, and your general process to fulfill it.

And again - this does <u>not</u> mean you're going to teach everyone how to do your job, or invite people to meddle in your stuff, or get everyone hopeful about becoming your replacement.

You'll just make sure that what goes on behind your closed office door isn't a mystery to anyone. And once that happens, you'll have a building full of people who can help you reach your fullest potential.

day 79 checklist

_____ do your morning ritual

_____ smile at yourself in the mirror

_____ do something active

_____ don't consume negative news

_____ listen to something positive, inspirational or instructional

_____ whenever someone irritates you, practice controlling your response

_____ do something you love

_____ do what you wrote down on DAY 40, to be a leader, and what you wrote on DAY 45, to become who you need to be to realize the company's vision

_____ think about how to help everyone to learn each other's job descriptions

_____ think about how to help everyone to learn your job description

add this if it's a **work day:**

_____ smile at, and greet every person you pass today at work

_____ give yourself and your employees some DO NOT DISTURB time

_____ be in character and include being purposefully-positive

_____ make all emails you send to employees follow DAY 33

_____ help your employees to be more active at work

_____ do whatever you identified to be better in your role for your employees

_____ listen to everyone's input, before you give your own

_____ help everyone to get over their fear of rejection around sales

day 80

After brainstorming for the last couple days, make a plan for how you could help everyone to learn both each other's and your responsibilities. Write it out, put it in your calendar, and set up any automatic reminders. Even if this isn't something you can get in place before the end of the challenge, just make sure it doesn't get forgotten.

day 80 checklist

_____ do your morning ritual

_____ smile at yourself in the mirror

_____ do something active

_____ don't consume negative news

_____ listen to something positive, inspirational or instructional

_____ whenever someone irritates you, practice controlling your response

_____ do something you love

_____ do what you wrote down on DAY 40, to be a leader, and what you wrote on DAY 45, to become who you need to be to realize the company's vision

_____ make a plan for how you might be able to help everyone to learn each other's job descriptions, as well as your own. Write it out, put it on your calendar, and set up automatic reminders.

add this if it's a **work day:**

_____ smile at, and greet every person you pass today at work

_____ give yourself and your employees some DO NOT DISTURB time

_____ be in character and include being purposefully-positive

_____ make all emails you send to employees follow DAY 33

_____ help your employees to be more active at work

_____ do whatever you identified to be better in your role for your employees

_____ listen to everyone's input, before you give your own

_____ help everyone to get over their fear of rejection around sales

day 81

Think about how you might be able to give everyone a little more freedom. You've set yourself up to make it a smoother process, after everything you put in place after DAY 18. And all those things you did to prevent (or end) micromanaging already went a long way to give your employees the independence they crave.

But just do some brainstorming today, and see if you can come up with any more ways to loosen the reigns a little. Maybe some positions could have deadlines for their work, instead of hours to work in. Maybe some could have shorter workdays. Or the ability to pick their own projects. Or maybe you could tell everyone the results you want, and let them deliver those in their own way.

If you decide on something, schedule any necessary preparation and set up reminders.

_____

_____

_____

_____

_____

_____

day 81 checklist

_____ do your morning ritual

_____ smile at yourself in the mirror

_____ do something active

_____ don't consume negative news

_____ listen to something positive, inspirational or instructional

_____ whenever someone irritates you, practice controlling your response

_____ do something you love

_____ do what you wrote down on DAY 40, to be a leader, and what you wrote on DAY 45, to become who you need to be to realize the company's vision

_____ think about ways to give everyone more freedom, and schedule anything you decide to move forward on

add this if it's a **work day:**

_____ smile at, and greet every person you pass today at work

_____ give yourself and your employees some DO NOT DISTURB time

_____ be in character and include being purposefully-positive

_____ make all emails you send to employees follow DAY 33

_____ help your employees to be more active at work

_____ do whatever you identified to be better in your role for your employees

_____ listen to everyone's input, before you give your own

_____ help everyone to get over their fear of rejection around sales

day 82

My client's voice was muffled.

"Can you use a little extra scrub on my back? I'll be wearing a strappy dress tomorrow and I really want my skin to look nice."

I flapped the wooden scoop in my hands. When my coworker trained me she'd demonstrated this service with a certain amount of product, and I'd already used that much. …But I wanted to keep my client happy. I wanted to go above-and-beyond, and give her a service she would rave about (and tip me well for).

Eh – shouldn't be a big deal. Day spas were about pampering, right? I plopped another blob of sea salt scrub onto her back and got to work.

At the end of her appointment, she tipped me happily and booked another one. And for the rest of the time I worked at that place, she expected me to use extra product with her services.

You don't need me to tell you that you lose money when people wander outside their scope of work. So let's skip to the point of today:

Think about what your company already has in place to ensure that everyone thoroughly understands and sticks with the scope, and think about what you might be able to do to improve on it. It could be with things like:

> Written procedures that clearly explain parameters, and the requirements for going outside of them (since in some cases it can be necessary).

> A form to be filled out for each project, with a place for the exact scope of work (unique to that project), along with details on specific things NOT to do.

> Training meetings with common scenarios explained, and any questions answered.

> Labels on or under products that clearly state the exact amount to be used.

> Specifically-sized scoops/spoons/cups, etc., for each type of product.

> Pre-measured products.

Think about how you can make it easier for your employees to make the right choice in the moment, when time is crunched, a client is demanding, and there's no support or witnesses.

Think about the times it might be necessary to go outside the scope of work, and the procedures that would have to be followed to ensure billing is accurate, and unnecessary liability is avoided. Then think about what you can put in place to make it easier for those procedures to be followed.

Again – I probably don't need to make a case about why this is important, and I know you already have things in place. But while we're making time for improvements, let's see if there's any to be made here.

Tomorrow we'll talk about something that might help you with this whole subject.

day 82 checklist

_____ do your morning ritual

_____ smile at yourself in the mirror

_____ do something active

_____ don't consume negative news

_____ listen to something positive, inspirational or instructional

_____ whenever someone irritates you, practice controlling your response

_____ do something you love

_____ do what you wrote down on DAY 40, to be a leader, and what you wrote on DAY 45, to become who you need to be to realize the company's vision

_____ think about how you might help everyone to stick to the scope of work

add this if it's a **work day:**

_____ smile at, and greet every person you pass today at work

_____ give yourself and your employees some DO NOT DISTURB time

_____ be in character and include being purposefully-positive

_____ make all emails you send to employees follow DAY 33

_____ help your employees to be more active at work

_____ do whatever you identified to be better in your role for your employees

_____ listen to everyone's input, before you give your own

_____ help everyone to get over their fear of rejection around sales

day 83

Consider starting a profit share plan.

Yesterday we talked about helping everyone to stick to the scope of work on every project, and on DAY 19 and DAY 81 we talked about helping everyone to do their jobs with more independence, and this is the perfect way to help them all to avoid waste, excess spending and unnecessary liability, and you won't have to lose your voice going on about it, or perch on every shoulder.

I love profit share plans. They're a great way to thank your employees, to help them feel personally invested in the company's results, and to motivate everyone to make good choices. And it's just so nice to give back a little more to the people who make it all happen.

And profit share plans are so customizable. You can set one up that really works for your company. You can set it up so that you have peace of mind, and your company's interest is protected.

You can get your financial advice from an expert, so this is all I'll say about your actual plan:

(1) You'll pick a time frame to measure and pay out on.

There's pros and cons to shorter or longer ones. A shorter time period means smaller amounts to pay out at once, and people getting rewards more often, but it can also mean some expenses might trickle in late, and maybe the exact numbers won't be quite as accurate (although you can just adjust the next payout to correct any inaccuracies from the previous one, etc.). And maybe smaller rewards will be less exciting to people (depending on the actual amounts).

A longer time period means the numbers will probably be more accurate. And it means there will be a bigger amount to pay out all at once. That might be exciting to employees, but the length of time might also make it hard for people to remember every day.

There's more to consider with the time-frame, but those were just some examples. And once you go over them and decide what's best, you'll probably have something like once a month, or once a quarter, or once a year. Or once per project. Or a totally customized length of time that works with the cycles of your business.

I know a business owner who pays out a certain percentage on the total net profit every quarter, plus a higher percentage of the total net profit of each completed project. You might decide on something similar, so that you have more incentives working for you at once.

(2) **You'll decide what to pay out on.** If you don't want to white-knuckle your way through the ebbs of your cash flow, you'll always pay out on net profits.

But you can also customize it even more. You might decide to go through your Chart of Accounts and look at certain trends in expense categories, and decide that they need to stay within a certain acceptable limit. Or you might look at your income and decide that you'll pay out even more on certain types of sales.

(3) **You'll decide on a percentage, and how that will be distributed.** You might pick a percentage and divide it up evenly across the board, or you might give different percentages according to position.

At a company I used to work at, every employee participated in the profit share plan, but certain positions got a higher percentage. At another company I know of, the profit share percentage is split evenly with all employees, regardless of position.

As you're thinking about the actual amount, consider starting conservatively. You can always thrill everyone later by upping the percentage, but taking it back won't go over well. One business owner I know started by having all of his employees split half of a percentage, and he increased the number over time.

(4) **You'll decide who participates.** I'd suggest making this a company-wide thing, and available to all employees, regardless of positions. You want people at every level working hard to increase profits.

But you might decide on certain factors for employees to qualify. Maybe after an employee has been with the company for at least 90 days. Maybe as long as there have been no write-ups for non-compliance of policies during that period.

(5) **You'll decide on any other customization.** Maybe full-time employees will get a higher percentage than part-time (I will just toss out that I think part-time employees should still be able to participate, even if you decide on a lower percentage). Maybe when people have been with the company for a certain amount of time, you'll up their percentage. Maybe people who prove to be higher performers over a certain amount of time will get a higher percentage.

(6) **Put it in place and give it a trial run**, so you can see how it goes and adjust as necessary. (But like I mentioned before, I'd start conservatively, so any adjustments will also feel like an improvement for the employees.)

Like I said, that's the basics, but you can always get an actual professional in this area to help you get the right plan figured out.

I would just really give this some thought, because it's such a win-win. If you already have a profit share plan in place, evaluate it today and think about anything you might do to improve it and make it even more mutually-beneficial.

And I know – there is plenty of research out there suggesting that a profit share plan by itself won't perform miracles, but you aren't making it your only strategy. I think layered in with all the other things you're putting in place, it'll make your company all the more appealing to quality candidates, and the quality employees you want to retain.

And I think it'll give further support to the things you're doing for all of your current employees, to motivate them, show them appreciation, give them independence, and help them to be vigilant when it comes to the important details.

The right plan will be an investment that ultimately pays out the most to your company every time, so take some time today to consider it, and put any reminders you need in your calendar.

day 83 checklist

_____ do your morning ritual

_____ smile at yourself in the mirror

_____ do something active

_____ don't consume negative news

_____ listen to something positive, inspirational or instructional

_____ whenever someone irritates you, practice controlling your response

_____ do something you love

_____ do what you wrote down on DAY 40, to be a leader, and what you wrote on DAY 45, to become who you need to be to realize the company's vision

_____ consider starting a profit share plan, and set up any reminders you need for further planning & executing

add this if it's a **work day:**

_____ smile at, and greet every person you pass today at work

_____ give yourself and your employees some DO NOT DISTURB time

_____ be in character and include being purposefully-positive

_____ make all emails you send to employees follow DAY 33

_____ help your employees to be more active at work

_____ do whatever you identified to be better in your role for your employees

_____ listen to everyone's input, before you give your own

_____ help everyone to get over their fear of rejection around sales

day 84

My boss and coworker were arguing.

"You were supposed to have the lead on this! You can't let things slip through the cracks!"

"Look, I *did* have the lead on it, and then *you* jumped in. You told me that you were going to the meeting instead, and then I didn't hear about the changes they decided on, and then you kept working on it without me."

I was hovering over my computer, trying to look absorbed in my work and hanging on every word. I'd heard similar arguments between coworkers in almost every job I'd been in, and I had found myself in this type of mix-up more than once. And here it was, playing out ten feet away with my boss involved.

His shoulders were slumped. "Well – I know. But I thought you got sent the details on that."

"And I thought you wanted to take over, so I let you."

I know I've been going on about turning your company into a fairyland of love, with people who flutter around to have each other's backs. But anything can be taken too far, and done in the wrong way, so today we're going to get everybody back to their own desks, and keep them out of each other's way.

It's time to eliminate dabbling, which is completely different than being helpful. You don't want people jumping in and out of each other's responsibilities and making a big mixed-up mess. You don't want projects that are partially started, then discarded when normal duties call. You don't want arguments over who really "should" have done something, and at what point the screw-up began. You don't want confusion and false expectations over who will take charge and come to the rescue. And you don't want mistakes and mishaps, when people who aren't familiar with something try to pitch in and take over.

You want organization. You want roles that are clearly defined, and responsibilities that are separated. Here's how you'll do it:

(1) **Make lists of each job title and its responsibilities.** Include how those responsibilities coordinate with other positions, and where those overlap. This will go along perfectly with what you did on DAY 78, and with the written procedures

manuals we talked about on DAY 19.

(2) **Make a written procedure for collaboration** – because this doesn't mean there can't be any. You just want organization when people decide to share and work together. You'll want to make a way for it to be clear each time, as far as who is ultimately responsible for the results of each aspect of the work.

(3) **Make the lists and procedures accessible to each person** (again, this could be saved as part of the procedures manual for that position).

(4) **Let everyone know what you've been working on, and what it means.** You might do it with a meeting, or an email (just make sure it gets read by each person), or by communicating it to managers who will spread the word.

(5) **Be diligent about following your plan, and helping managers to follow it.** It would be easy to accidentally send someone into foreign territory when you're just trying to hurry up and get it all done. It'll take vigilance, and diligence, and patience, and good judgement.

And again – this does not mean people can't collaborate, and help each other out. It's just that you want all of that done in an organized way, so things get completed fully, and with accuracy, and with quality. You want teamwork without the misunderstandings, and bickering, and dropped balls.

 This also doesn't mean there can't be change, or that people can't grow and evolve. You just want change to be organized, and clearly defined, and in writing (ideally).

I had a boss who got really serious about this. He drew a map of every position, and the associated job description, and the intersections with other positions and job descriptions. He sat us all down for a meeting where he showed us his drawing, and explained the potential pitfalls if we all tried to wear every hat. He clearly defined our roles, and gave us procedures for collaborating, and then he asked us to remind him about this if he got busy one day and approached one of us with a task that wasn't our business.

I went back to work after the meeting, and I saw the difference that day. And over the next week the improvements became more and more apparent. The amount of times I was getting interrupted were cut at least in half. I knew exactly who to go to when I had a question about a certain area of a project. My coworkers and I were able to work more efficiently together. I was completely clear about what was expected of me, and I knew what to prioritize. I was able to quickly delegate a list of miscellaneous work that I hadn't known what to do with before. I was way more accurate, I got work done faster, and my stress level plummeted.

This will make everyone work better together, and work better for you. Give it some thought and planning today, and then make space on your calendar, so you can finish putting whatever-you-need-to in place.

day 84 checklist

_____ do your morning ritual

_____ smile at yourself in the mirror

_____ do something active

_____ don't consume negative news

_____ listen to something positive, inspirational or instructional

_____ whenever someone irritates you, practice controlling your response

_____ do something you love

_____ do what you wrote down on DAY 40, to be a leader, and what you wrote on DAY 45, to become who you need to be to realize the company's vision

_____ think about how you can help everyone to have more clearly-defined roles, separated responsibilities, and organized collaboration

add this if it's a **work day:**

_____ smile at, and greet every person you pass today at work

_____ give yourself and your employees some DO NOT DISTURB time

_____ be in character and include being purposefully-positive

_____ make all emails you send to employees follow DAY 33

_____ help your employees to be more active at work

_____ do whatever you identified to be better in your role for your employees

_____ listen to everyone's input, before you give your own

_____ help everyone to get over their fear of rejection around sales

notes & ideas

week 13

week 13 checklist

here's what you'll do at least 1 time each this week

____ ask an employee, "how are you?", and then listen to the answer, give a thoughtful response, and follow up later (if applicable)

____ sincerely thank an employee for his/her unique contribution to the company (you want everyone who works for you – or at least those you can come in contact with – to hear this from you by the end of the challenge)

____ ____ ____ prepare to work on a personal goal the next morning

____ ____ ____ work on a personal goal first thing in the morning

____ do random acts of kindness for your employees

____ visit your employees around work, and ask how they're doing and if there's anything they need

____ write and mail a letter to an employee, thanking him/her for being part of the company, expressing specific things he/she has done well, his/her strengths, and things you admire about the employee's character (write enough of these each week so that all employees have received one from you by the end of the challenge)

____ work at connecting each employee with a person you know who could give advice/be a mentor/etc. for that employee's personal goal (your list is on DAY 63)

day 85

I saw something like this in a book, I think it's so brilliant, and today we'll put our own spin on it, to support what we already talked about on DAY 75:

Think about today's accomplishments; things involving production, or marketing, or research and development, etc. Things that got completed today, that you could measure. And when you do this, focus on your employees' positive actions. You'll need to factor in the results if you're looking at things like specific work completed (because it'll need to be done with quality), but try not to make this about the number of sales made today.

Decide what you'll measure, and then write that total number, gigantic and bold, where everyone will see it. You don't even have to give an explanation for the number until someone asks, and then you'll tell them, "it's the total number of units we assembled today", or "it's the total number of prospects we called on today," or "it's the total number of add-on services we offered today," or whatever it represents.

Then you can say, "Let's see what we can do tomorrow."

Change the number tomorrow, and repeat this for the rest of the time of this challenge. Then at the end, congratulate everyone, and if you're happy with how it all went, consider whether you want to make it a regular thing.

day 85 checklist

_____ do your morning ritual

_____ smile at yourself in the mirror

_____ do something active

_____ don't consume negative news

_____ listen to something positive, inspirational or instructional

_____ whenever someone irritates you, practice controlling your response

_____ do something you love

_____ do what you wrote down on DAY 40, to be a leader, and what you wrote on DAY 45, to become who you need to be to realize the company's vision

add this if it's a work day:

_____ smile at, and greet every person you pass today at work

_____ give yourself and your employees some DO NOT DISTURB time

_____ be in character and include being purposefully-positive

_____ make all emails you send to employees follow DAY 33

_____ help your employees to be more active at work

_____ do whatever you identified to be better in your role for your employees

_____ listen to everyone's input, before you give your own

_____ help everyone to get over their fear of rejection around sales

_____ measure today's accomplishments, write the number for all to see, and repeat for the rest of the challenge

day 86

Prioritize your employees' safety today. I've heard some really compelling things about how much this can positively affect the performance and success of an entire company, and whether that sounds like a stretch to you or not, none of us can deny how devastating one accident can be, or the potential consequences of one report of negligence.

I'm sure you've already got safety measures in place, but give this some time today anyway, and see if there are any areas that could improve.

Make sure you've got first aid kits and supplies available, and that everyone knows where those are.

Walk the whole building, and make sure there aren't any hidden hazards.

Think about each step of each procedure, and how you might make it safer, if needed.

Make sure no one can do any work with machinery, chemicals, hot-anything, or sharp tools while taking pain medicine after getting a tooth pulled, or while still buzzing from a late-night party.

Make sure you've got written procedures for accidents/injuries that include instructions to prioritize getting help for injured employees, how to report the incident, and which positions are responsible for which steps of the process. Make sure each person has access to those written procedures and all necessary forms, and has been given face-to-face instructions.

Consider whether yours is an industry where you'd need to hold regular, documented safety meetings and trainings. If so, start the process of gathering topics and sign-in forms for each individual meeting, making a place for those documents, and deciding on a schedule and presenters.

If you don't have an official written safety policy, start having that drafted, and make sure a completed copy is given to each employee.

If you don't have a Drug Free Workplace policy, consider whether your company should, and look into how to start that process.

Consider whether yours is an industry or type of work that would benefit from having someone in a full-time Safety Coordinator position.

This could end up requiring more time than just today, so put anything you need to into your calendar, and set up any reminders.

And again – I'm sure you've already got things in place, but a little vigilance today can't hurt. You might find one simple thing to improve, and it might prevent a catastrophe down the road.

And no, this doesn't mean you have to put your office employees in padded suits and helmets, require fall protection harnesses when taking the stairs, and replace all the scissors with the ones your five-year-old uses in class.

You can be practical, and level-headed about the whole thing, and you can treat your adults like grown-ups, and you can take steps as the business is ready for them.

I just think that in addition to preventing potential tragedies and colossal expenses, your investment in this area will go a long way to show everyone you care about them. So let's give this time today.

day 86 checklist

_____ do your morning ritual

_____ smile at yourself in the mirror

_____ do something active

_____ don't consume negative news

_____ listen to something positive, inspirational or instructional

_____ whenever someone irritates you, practice controlling your response

_____ do something you love

_____ do what you wrote down on DAY 40, to be a leader, and what you wrote on DAY 45, to become who you need to be to realize the company's vision

_____ think about how your employee safety policy/measures might be improved

add this if it's a **work day:**

_____ smile at, and greet every person you pass today at work

_____ give yourself and your employees some DO NOT DISTURB time

_____ be in character and include being purposefully-positive

_____ make all emails you send to employees follow DAY 33

_____ help your employees to be more active at work

_____ do whatever you identified to be better in your role for your employees

_____ listen to everyone's input, before you give your own

_____ help everyone to get over their fear of rejection around sales

_____ measure today's accomplishments and write the number for all to see

day 87

Do some research today into "how to lead different generations in the workplace". Read/watch/listen to at least three things, and write down the ideas they gave you. Then identify one thing you can do starting now, put a circle around it, and get started the next time you're with everyone at work.

day 87 checklist

_____ do your morning ritual

_____ smile at yourself in the mirror

_____ do something active

_____ don't consume negative news

_____ listen to something positive, inspirational or instructional

_____ whenever someone irritates you, practice controlling your response

_____ do something you love

_____ do what you wrote down on DAY 40, to be a leader, and what you wrote on DAY 45, to become who you need to be to realize the company's vision

_____ research "how to lead different generations in the workplace", write down your ideas, and identify one thing to start doing now

add this if it's a **work day:**

_____ smile at, and greet every person you pass today at work

_____ give yourself and your employees some DO NOT DISTURB time

_____ be in character and include being purposefully-positive

_____ make all emails you send to employees follow DAY 33

_____ help your employees to be more active at work

_____ do whatever you identified to be better in your role for your employees

_____ listen to everyone's input, before you give your own

_____ help everyone to get over their fear of rejection around sales

_____ measure today's accomplishments and write the number for all to see

day 88

Give your employees an optional challenge:

Ask everyone who would like to participate to prepare a (predetermined length) presentation on a cause or charity they're passionate about, to be delivered to you and all their coworkers on the day of your choice.

If you want to take it a little further, you could decide beforehand how much money you can afford to give in total if each person does the presentation, then divide that by the number of employees, and tell everyone you'll contribute that amount of money to each cause presented. Or find some other way to work out contributing (like by giving a certain percentage of sales in a month to one of the charities, until each one had a turn, etc.).

If your company has a blog or other social media sites, you could post pictures of the presentations, along with a description of each person's chosen cause, and how others can contribute.

Besides developing everyone's presentation skills, this will give them all a great feeling about you, about each other, and about being part of your company – whether they choose to present something or not. You'll all be inspired together, and get a great feeling of fulfillment and belief in mankind together, while you learn about caring people who strive to make the world a better place, and how you can each join in their efforts. It'll be such a great experience, you might even decide to make it a regular thing.

day 88 checklist

_____ do your morning ritual

_____ smile at yourself in the mirror

_____ do something active

_____ don't consume negative news

_____ listen to something positive, inspirational or instructional

_____ whenever someone irritates you, practice controlling your response

_____ do something you love

_____ do what you wrote down on DAY 40, to be a leader, and what you wrote on DAY 45, to become who you need to be to realize the company's vision

add this if it's a **work day:**

_____ smile at, and greet every person you pass today at work

_____ give yourself and your employees some DO NOT DISTURB time

_____ be in character and include being purposefully-positive

_____ make all emails you send to employees follow DAY 33

_____ help your employees to be more active at work

_____ do whatever you identified to be better in your role for your employees

_____ listen to everyone's input, before you give your own

_____ help everyone to get over their fear of rejection around sales

_____ measure today's accomplishments and write the number for all to see

_____ give your employees the (optional) challenge to prepare a presentation on a cause/charity of their choice, to be given on your chosen date

_____ schedule the date and time for your employees' presentations, put that in your calendar, send out to the employees, and set up any automatic reminders you need

_____ do what you wrote on DAY 87, to effectively lead different generations

day 89

Make a post on your company's social media site about your gratitude for the wonderful people you work with (your employees).

Really think about it beforehand, so you can make it sincere. Go back to DAY 2 and read the list you made, think about each person there, and get your cup running over with thankful feelings.

Then make your post, and express a heartfelt thanks.

day 89 checklist

_____ do your morning ritual

_____ smile at yourself in the mirror

_____ do something active

_____ don't consume negative news

_____ listen to something positive, inspirational or instructional

_____ whenever someone irritates you, practice controlling your response

_____ do something you love

_____ do what you wrote down on DAY 40, to be a leader, and what you wrote on DAY 45, to become who you need to be to realize the company's vision

_____ make a post to your company's social media site(s), expressing sincere gratitude for your employees

add this if it's a **work day:**

_____ smile at, and greet every person you pass today at work

_____ give yourself and your employees some DO NOT DISTURB time

_____ be in character and include being purposefully-positive

_____ make all emails you send to employees follow DAY 33

_____ help your employees to be more active at work

_____ do whatever you identified to be better in your role for your employees

_____ listen to everyone's input, before you give your own

_____ help everyone to get over their fear of rejection around sales

_____ measure today's accomplishments and write the number for all to see

_____ do what you wrote on DAY 87, to effectively lead different generations

day 90

Here's what you'll do for this last day of the challenge:

Read the article, "How to make your employees love you". You'll recognize everything in it; they're all things you've been purposefully doing during this challenge, and the article will be a great summary to wrap this all up.

Here's the link:

https://prosky.co/talkingtalent/articles/how-to-make-your-employees-love-you-increasing-engagement-and-retention

Then – you did it! You did all ninety days of the challenge! Pat yourself on the back, go do something to celebrate, and enjoy the relief. ...Just don't close the book and put it away yet.

day 90 checklist

_____ do your morning ritual

_____ smile at yourself in the mirror

_____ do something active

_____ don't consume negative news

_____ listen to something positive, inspirational or instructional

_____ whenever someone irritates you, practice controlling your response

_____ do something you love

_____ do what you wrote down on DAY 40, to be a leader, and what you wrote on DAY 45, to become who you need to be to realize the company's vision

_____ read the article, "How to make your employees love you"

add this if it's a **work day:**

_____ smile at, and greet every person you pass today at work

_____ give yourself and your employees some DO NOT DISTURB time

_____ be in character and include being purposefully-positive

_____ make all emails you send to employees follow DAY 33

_____ help your employees to be more active at work

_____ do whatever you identified to be better in your role for your employees

_____ listen to everyone's input, before you give your own

_____ help everyone to get over their fear of rejection around sales

_____ measure today's accomplishments, write the number for all to see, and then celebrate the actions everyone has taken during the last five days

_____ do what you wrote on DAY 87, to effectively lead different generations

notes & ideas

day 91+

You just spent a whole quarter of the year putting great things in place, and if this was a different type of challenge you might be able to hit the breaks at this point. But it's not, and you can't, so you'll have to keep in mind what we went over in the introduction, and on DAY 50:

Consistency is *essential*.

You can't abandon everything now, or all of your hard work could actually backfire, and you've put in too much effort to let that happen. You are *so* well on your way to having a company full of people who make it the place of your dreams, so let's keep going, and I've made some things to help you.

The next four pages have lists for you. Tear them out of the book, laminate or frame them, put them up where you'll see them every day, and then use a dry-erase marker to keep track of your progress.

There are four checklists: things you'll need to continue doing every single day, things to do every work day, things to do at least once a week, and things to do consistently.

There's also a list of long-term projects from the challenge that you may not have had a chance to complete or put in place yet, so I included the DAY Number, so you can go back and reference it when you make your plan.

Go ahead and tear those pages out now, and then I'll show you what's next.

to do daily

_____ do your morning ritual

_____ smile at yourself in the mirror

_____ do something active

_____ don't consume negative news

_____ listen to something positive, inspirational or instructional

_____ whenever someone irritates you, practice controlling your response

_____ do something you love

_____ do what you wrote down on DAY 40, to be a leader, and what you wrote on DAY 45, to become who you need to be to realize the company's vision

add this if it's a **work day**:

_____ smile at, and greet every person you pass today at work

_____ give yourself and your employees some DO NOT DISTURB time

_____ be in character and include being purposefully-positive

_____ make all emails you send to employees follow DAY 33

_____ help your employees to be more active at work

_____ do whatever you identified to be better in your role for your employees

_____ listen to everyone's input, before you give your own

_____ do what you wrote on DAY 87, to effectively lead different generations

AS ITS PEOPLE

to do weekly

_____ ask an employee, "how are you?", and then listen to the answer, give a thoughtful response, and follow up later (if applicable)

_____ _____ _____ prepare to work on a personal goal the next morning

_____ _____ _____ work on a personal goal first thing in the morning

_____ do random acts of kindness for your employees

_____ visit your employees around work, and ask how they're doing and if there's anything they need

AS ITS PEOPLE

to do regularly & consistently

_____ help your employees' jobs support their personal goals (*from DAY 8 & DAY 15*)

_____ help your employees support each other's personal goals (*from DAY 9*)

_____ keep DAY 10 in mind while you help your employees to achieve company goals

_____ make your position support your personal goals (*from DAY 16*)

_____ keep working on ways to let your employees do their jobs independently (*from DAY 18-20*)

_____ get to know your employees and find ways to show you care about them and the things that are important to them (*from DAY 22*)

_____ keep working on ways to help each of your employees show off their other talents at work (*reference lists made on DAY 29 & DAY 32*)

_____ look for ways to give recognition for assignments/projects (*from DAY 41*)

_____ use rewards effectively (*from DAY 42*)

_____ follow through on your employee wellness plan (*from DAY 44*)

_____ follow through on your employee development plan (*from DAY 46*)

_____ be consistent - and make sure management is too (*from DAY 50*)

_____ know what to do about low-performers (*from DAY 51*)

_____ follow through on your program to recognize and reward kindness (*from DAY 57*)

_____ do whatever you can to regularly give back as a company (*from DAY 59*)

_____ give back regularly in your personal life (*from DAY 60*)

_____ maximize your performance evaluations (*from DAY 62*)

_____ celebrate quality work getting done - not the time spent on it (*from DAY 64*)

_____ do your employee highlights(*from DAY 66*)

_____ learn how each of your employees is motivated and tailor your language (from DAY 67)

_____ learn your employees' values, and help their jobs to align with them (*from DAY 68 & 69*)

AS ITS PEOPLE

long-term projects

put things in place to help employees work with independence (*from DAY 18 – 20*)

make an employee wellness plan (*from DAY 44*)

make an employee development plan (*from DAY 46*)

write and mail a letter to each employee, thanking him/her for being part of the company, expressing specific things he/she has done well, his/her strengths, and things you admire about the employee's character (*from DAY 49*)

make a program for recognizing & rewarding kindness (*from DAY 57*)

work at connecting each employee with a person you know who could give advice/be a mentor/etc. for that employee's personal goal (*your list is on DAY 63*)

highlight each employee (*from DAY 66*)

think about how you might start helping your employee's jobs to align with their values (*from DAY 69*)

have the employees write what the mission statement means to them, and then display the answers in some way (*from DAY 70*)

plan something fun and unexpected to do for your employees (*from DAY 76*)

help employees to learn yours and their coworkers' responsibilities and how to support those (*from DAY 80*)

think of ways to give everyone more freedom (*from DAY 81*)

help everyone to understand & stick to the scope of work (from DAY 82)

consider a profit share plan (*from DAY 83*)

think about how you can help everyone to have more clearly-defined roles, separated responsibilities, and a plan for organized collaboration (*from DAY 84*)

think about how to improve on employee safety policy/methods (*from DAY 86*)

have employees plan an optional presentation on a cause/charity of their choice (*from DAY 88*)

AS ITS PEOPLE

bonus challenge

There's no time limit for this. Make it a longer-term thing you plan for and work toward.

Give your employees an adventure.

Want to wake everyone up, give them energy and confidence, and have them come back into work feeling like superstars? Think of a way to let them prove their awesomeness to themselves and each other.

Find a rock climbing course (even if it's indoors), or a boxing course, or archery, or shooting, or wilderness survival – and pay them to take it. It could be a one-day thing or a week, but you want to get everyone's adrenaline pumping and have them come back to the office feeling proud and impressed with themselves, and with their coworkers.

If this isn't something you can swing right now, you can make it a goal that you all work toward. Tell everyone you want to do this for them, and tell them that every time the company makes a certain amount in sales, you're going to put aside whatever-amount, and save it for this trip or whatever the specific adventure is.

You can also personalize this, and make it so the office isn't cleared out for a week. You could have each employee write down the adventure he/she would like (after you specify the length of time, and the kind of thing you're talking about – and you could even give a list of choices), and then when you have the sales to support it, schedule each person's thing so they aren't all taken at the same time.

Yes, you'll have liability issues to consider, and logistics to iron out, but I really think you could make something so special with this, that all of the work and expense to see it through would be so worth it.

And because you'll want to make sure you get the right plan in place, and since there's a lot to prepare for, this is back here, as a bonus, and you should take your time with it.

notes & ideas

The employees you already have can transform your company.

They each have so much potential, and you can bring it out, and help them become who they really can be.

You don't have to wait around, and go insane, on a merry-go-round ride of hiring, getting let down, firing, and starting all over. You don't have to cover your eyes and hope that people will decide to change themselves, or finally wake up one day and *get it*.

The biggest thing I want you to take from all this is that if we each felt truly confident in ourselves, and knew what we were worth, and knew that the people around us knew our worth, and really cared for us, we'd contribute so much more to whatever place we were in.

Who knows whether all of your employees get the kind of love and support and encouragement they need when they're at home. Who knows what life has told them about themselves and what they're capable of. Who knows what their experiences have made them believe about the world, and other peoples' motives, and what's possible for their lives.

So what if you decided to take action yourself? What if you decided to make your place truly special, and unique? What if - while other businesses in your industry put all their focus on customers, stakeholders, products, and numbers – what if you made the *people in the business* your focus? What if you made it so they come to work and get what the rest of their life doesn't give, or hasn't given them?

Don't you think they'd likely give you so much in return? It sounds like such mushy stuff, but if you really think about it, it's so practical.

And no – this doesn't mean you won't ever have trouble with employees again. And yeah – your place is a business, and you can't lose sight of that. You'll have to remember what we talked about on DAY 51. It's so much to navigate, and balance all at once, but that's part of your responsibility, and you can do it.

And when you figure it out, and find your groove with leading people this way, *you'll* have so much happiness, and so much fulfillment from your position. You'll love your business even more; it'll have even more meaning for you. You could make something legendary; something with a magic so far beyond whatever it actually does or sells.

So keep going.

Make your company with its people.

ABOUT THE AUTHOR

Joan ("Joanie") Elmore is a part-time employee with a mission to end the Sunday Night Blues and start a new way of working.

She uses what she's learned from her experience to help employees have happiness, fulfillment, and high-performance in their jobs, with a revolutionary approach to goal achievement.

Learn more at: useyourjob.com/about

Get the 90-day challenge for employees here: amazon.com/author/joanelmore

Made in the USA
Columbia, SC
17 January 2019